EDGAR R. TREXLER

Mission in a New World

FORTRESS PRESS   Philadelphia

All photographs by the author except page viii by Wallowitch
and page 75 by M. Gerald Arthur.

Library of Congress Catalog Number 76-62613

ISBN 0-8006-1257-4

6250A77   Printed in U.S.A.   1-1257

Cover Photo: *Waiting for a bus in Singapore*

To
my family,
which shares the vision
of a new world

Contents

Skyline of Dar es Salaam, capital of Tanzania

Introduction

One of every four persons on earth is Christian. That makes Christianity the largest and most universal religious grouping in the world, a remarkable record since it was begun by One who lived not quite two thousand years ago. He was the One who promised that even though his message fell among thorns, rocks, and hardened soil, the harvest would be great. And it has.

But having one-fourth of the world's population as Christian means that the movement is still three-fourths short of 100 percent—the goal implied in the words, "Go into *all* the world. . . ." Christians ever since the disciples have been missionaries—some effective and some ineffective. All of us witness by commission or omission to all we meet. One cannot escape being a missionary regardless of where one lives.

And where one lives in today's world means that a book can analyze the setting for only a few years. Things change too rapidly for such words to be timeless. As recently as 1945, for example, more than 99 percent of the non-Western world was under western domination. But by 1970, the statistic was reversed with more than 99 percent of the non-Western world independent.

Just as these figures have changed, so this book builds upon my earlier work which began describing the "new face" of missions a few years ago. Now, as then, the images of India lace, jungles, and missionaries in Pearl Buck pith helmets have given way to missionaries who work and live as much in the world's cities as anywhere else—and generally in comfort. They are partners with the leaders of the overseas churches, following instructions from these leaders as much as giving them guidance. Sixteen percent of missionaries today spend only two or three years abroad in constrast with the former sainted, white-haired men and women who served a lifetime. And more missionaries today are lay than clergy.

What's more, the pluralism that has swept America is sweeping the mission enterprise but under a different name —cooperation, which includes the sharing of facilities, interfaith dialogues, criticism of the Western way of doing things, and bold steps into the arenas of politics and human rights.

The new world is a challenge to churches because it means "letting go" of much of the past and grasping a future where American missionaries will not call all the shots. Churches in the Third World are not only directing much of their own destiny; they are already influencing Western churches by sending missionaries to America and Europe. A new age of shared insights into the gospel is at our doorstep.

Unfortunately, some church members find that threatening. They also discover that the less exotic mission settings become, the less interested they are in supporting them. One's backdoor doesn't seem nearly as interesting as something far away. Trying to overcome that apathy is one reason why this book was written.

Another reason is to show faithful churchgoers that even though religion may seem to be faring poorly in America, astonishing progress is being made by churches in other parts of the world. Since America is a great country, far too many people believe that if great things are not happening for God's church in America, then great things cannot be happening for him anywhere. That's both narrow-minded and God-limiting.

Moreover, there's so much to be gained from a vision of a new world and of new mission approaches that it cannot be said once and dropped. It has to be repeated over and over. Some of the photographs in these pages may tell you more than some of the text. You'll find lots of anecdotes and illustrations, stories about people and their accomplishments, and explanations of new mission efforts and their challenges—and how these efforts fit into an urbanizing world. Without intending to sound presumptous, I would hope that the reader's view of the world's church might be altered through these pages.

I owe some debts for the material here. Literally hundreds of people have taken me into their homes, offices, churches, and hearts in the thirty-one countries I have visited in recent years. For these hospitalities I am grateful and trust that the words here are faithful to the way these people are carrying out the church's mission. There has been encouragement and assistance along the way from other sources—from Bill Dudde and Dave Vikner of the Lutheran Church in America's Division for World Mission and Ecumenism; from Al Stauderman, Carl Uehling and my other colleagues at The Lutheran; from my wife, Emily, and my children, David, Mark, and Karen, who have been patient and accommodating during my travels and writing. Thanks must also go to my secretaries, Rosella Wise and Dorothy Ritter, who have toiled faithfully with this and other manuscripts.

But these people, and those mentioned in the following pages, are also special because they are the "people of God." They are part of the one-quarter of the world's population who are Christian. To all of them—and to you and me as reader and writer—belongs the opportunity of a better understanding of how to reach the remaining three-fourths of this planet's occupants through a "mission in a new world."

EDGAR R. TREXLER

Philadelphia, Pennsylvania
February 1977

1 The World Is Our Home

In the middle of 1974, the newly oil-rich sheikdom of Kuwait purchased the 3,500-acre Kiawah Island off the coast of South Carolina for $17 million. Within weeks, the Arab government of the tiny Middle East country turned the property over to a firm noted for developing plush beach resorts. Almost as quickly, newspapers published headlines that the fourteen thousand poverty-level blacks living on neighboring Wadmalaw and John's Islands would be seeing Arabs in their financial future.

For more than a century, these black people had tilled small farms and fished muddy streams to survive. Most of their ancestors were slaves who were freed after the Civil War. Over the years, they had not been able to find financial security in a white-dominated world, including the Jewish population of nearby Charleston which had asked the blacks to help block the development of the Arab-owned resort. But now, thanks to the rich—and perhaps wise—men from the East, the blacks would for the first time in their history have an alternative to abject poverty.

Methodist minister Willis T. Goodwin who serves five island churches had a strong hand in getting the beach developers to agree that the black population of Wadmalaw and John's Islands would have the first opportunity at the estimated nine thousand jobs which would be created at the resort. The Arabs also agreed to give the islanders $9,000 yearly for three years to develop a community school to teach them marketable skills, and to build a "brickcrete" factory to manufacture low-cost building materials for inexpensive homes for island residents.

The Arab investment off the coast of South Carolina brings the development of our planet's "global village" dramatically to North American shores. For years, Americans have been aware of the investment of United States companies abroad. Many companies, such as Proctor and Gamble, General Motors, Ford, ITT, IBM, Chrysler, and Kodak employ more than one-third of their work force outside the United States. Some companies have plants in as many as twenty countries.

Some three hundred and sixty U. S. companies have a direct investment of more than $1.2 billion in South Africa, with the investments increasing by 12.8 percent each year. According to estimates by the United States Commerce Department, various multinational corporations control fifty-nine of the largest one hundred manufacturing concerns in Brazil. Such enterprises control 100 percent of Brazil's automobile production, 94 percent of the pharmaceutical industry, 91 percent of the tobacco industry, and 82 percent of rubber production.

The National Council of Churches reports that Gulf and Western is the largest landowner, employer, taxpayer, and exporter in the Dominican Republic, with assets there of about $200 million. At the same time, Gulf and Western pays sugarcane workers about $1 per day, with workers spending as much as 50 percent of their wages to pay mortgages on company-built housing.

In Italy, businessmen were shocked last year when the Libyan government purchased 10 percent of the assets of Fiat, the giant automobile manufacturer. Observers of Japan's commercial empire recall easily how two prime ministers were toppled as a result of that country's involvements with the financial scandals of the American multinational giant, Lockheed.

These examples suggest something that the intelligent man and woman of the future cannot ignore: The world is our home. The county in which we were born, the state in which we live, and even the country which we love cannot be the end of our horizon. Even if we never live abroad, virtually everything we touch—and that touches us—will be interwoven in the world's texture. If you need proof of that, pick up your nearest Sears and Roebuck catalogue. There you will note the following:

Stuffed animals made in Korea; denim jackets from Sri Lanka; raincoats with National Football League emblems made in Taiwan; girls' shoes from Spain, Italy, Taiwan, and Brazil; chain saws assembled in Mexico; warm-up jackets with boys' sizes made in Thailand or Korea, and students' sizes made in Columbia or the Philippines. There are hurricane lamps from Italy, badminton sets from Hong Kong, leisure jackets from Singapore, acrylic slippers from Puerto Rico, mantel clocks from West Germany, and the ever-present electronics products from Japan. My family has been amused that the souvenir White House we purchased in Washington has "Made in Japan" stamped on the bottom, and the miniature Lincoln Memorial says, "Made in Taiwan."

But these purchases are only the tip of the iceberg regarding our new home. Instant communications means that we saw the Vietnam War fought on television and sat spellbound in our living rooms while watching men walk on the moon. Rapid travel, both for business and pleasure, has mushroomed so greatly that the Rev. Ron O'Grady of New Zealand told a gathering in Williamsburg, Va. last year that tourists had to be educated "in order that they may change their sterotypes, prejudices, and attitudes toward the developing nations."

The energy crisis has made Americans dependent upon Arab oil barons, and even if a U. S. policy of energy-sufficiency succeeds, the rest of the world will still have oil problems because countries like Holland and Japan depend heavily upon the Middle East for their supplies. American oil independence is not as good an idea for the world as some type of interdependence on fossil fuels. Then there are the international matters of peace and security. The United

States and Russia already have sufficient nuclear arsenals to destroy each other many times over, with estimates indicating that within nine years, thirty-five countries will be able to manufacture atomic weapons. We must either have peace for everyone or there is peace for no one. Interdependence, particularly with the urban boom confronting the world everywhere, is a necessity, not a luxury.

The Urban Crunch

Some 35 percent of the world's population today lives in cities. The continent of Europe needed two hundred years for urbanization to progress to its present point. By contrast, Asia has needed only sixty years to reach its level of urban life, and Africa has needed only twenty years. The urban population in the United States grows by 1 percent each year. In Africa, urban population grows by 10 percent yearly. By the year 2000, 45 percent of Africa's population will be in the cities. Already 50 percent of South Africans and Rhodesians live in urban areas, and 35 percent of Nigerians.

In Kano, Nigeria, for example, camel caravans still trek across the Sahara Desert to a watering hole inside the walled section of the old city. The drivers unload dates and potash and barter them for embroidered cloth. But beyond the walls of the old city, in the burgeoning commercial section, business men arrive daily by jet from Rome and Cairo, dine at the Magwam Water restaurant which has three chlorinated swimming pools and a miniature golf course, and haggle over multimillion dollar contracts.

When a jet approaches the airport at Dar es Salaam, the capital of Tanzania, a section of the city comes into view which looks much like the suburban sprawl of American cities. Hundreds of houses have been built close together, alike in appearance, and facing gently winding streets. The houses have zinc roofs, and the walls are made of cement blocks. This is middleclass housing in one of the city's new developments, only one of many indications that the quiet seaport of Dar es Salaam (which means "haven of peace") is being transformed into a city of traffic jams, skyscrapers, and bustling stores.

With its three hundred and thirty-five thousand population increasing by 10 percent each year, Dar es Salaam will need one hundred and seventy-five more primary schools, two thousand eight hundred more hospital beds, and two hundred and ten new churches within twenty years. The city already points proudly to the campus of the University of Tanzania where classroom buildings, a snack bar, professors' offices, landscape gardens, multistoried dormitories, and an auditorium with a rounded dome like an American coliseum gleam in the African sunshine. Visitors can stay at the air-conditioned Kilimanjaro Hotel, going to the rooftop discotheque at night or to the teletype in the lobby which clacks out the news of the world in English.

A few thousand miles away, the pattern of life in Saudi Arabia is becoming swifter as modern Saudis spend some of the country's 25 billion annual oil revenue. The new streets of the city of Jidda are frequently jammed with imported cars, many with shipping stickers still in their windows. Newspapers advertise such luxury items as Christian Dior shoes, French pate, Chanel perfumes, and Dutch cream. National Guardsmen who formerly bounced around in trucks are completing an American-run program that has transformed the Guard into a mechanized light infantry equipped with armored cars.

In Madras, India, fine stores and shops meet the eye on the left and the right. High-rise apartments dot the skyline. A large red hotel which is under construction has a sign out front, "Madras will soon be a little more wonderful." At the hotel where I stayed, I made several delightful discoveries: air-conditioning, an appetizing menu in the dining room, and Western music. The shrimp cocktail was $1.13; filet mignon $1.73; tossed salad 47¢; coffee 40¢. The complete meal was $3.73. The entertainment was by sitar. One of the three performers broke into a broad smile at the Americans in the dining room as he played "Love Story," "Do Re Mi" from *The Sound of Music,* and "Never on Sunday." During a drive through the city, I spotted a golf course—with sand greens instead of grass.

Now let the urban sweep move to Asia. In Singapore, two million people live on 224 square miles. Shops and people are jammed together, and horns beep and bicyclists weave as they make their way though the streets and sidewalks. For more than ten years, Singapore has been building high-rise apartments at the rate of twelve thousand units per year. The thousands of squatters huts and palm-leaf houses that once dotted the downtown area are gone. Today, one in every four Singaporeans lives in a flat, as the apartments are called. "With few resources available and the population increase, the apartment estates are a good answer to Singapore's housing problem," said John Nelson. "We think they're crowded, but the quality of life there is better than it was in the slums." (Pastor Nelson is now in Kuala Lampur, Malaysia.)

Even Boy Scouts are different in Singapore. The Minister for Education told the scouts that they should give up their traditional "jungle" activities and convert themselves into "good, useful city scouts." Apply yourselves, he said, to preparing for emergencies such as car crashes, elevator and escalator breakdowns, and water rationing. Some Singaporeans get nostalgic about the British colonial past of the island. But they also say, "You either make progress, which means more high-rise construction, wider roads, and more traffic, or you stay put—in which case there's less money in the pocket, more unemployment, and more trouble."

In many parts of the Far East, urban growth is almost legendary. Hong Kong had six hundred thousand residents in 1945. It now has four million. Grace Lutheran Church occupies a storefront like its neighboring shops, including one with a garish red and blue sign, "Whiskey Go-Go Bar" and a statue of a dancing girl in yellow shorts.

Most legendary, perhaps, is Tokyo with its eleven million people. The city overwhelmed me. When I went to the Shinjuku railroad station at rush hour people overwhelmed me. I tried to go down the stairs to where the train was waiting, but the people who had come into the station on the train were swarming up the stairs and I had to wait. Politicians who like to "press the flesh" would love this station.

I was overwhelmed by Tokyo's expressways. Some of the intersections look like spaghetti—and I've never seen so many Toyotas! And I am overwhelmed by Tokyo's prices! I went to a meat market and noticed that steak cost 500 yen per 100 grams. I asked the butcher how many grams were in a pound. He said 454 grams. I already knew that 500 yen equalled $1.92. That means one quarter pound cost $1.92. Or $9.00 per pound.

I was overwhelmed by Tokyo's diversity: houses, trees, glass-walled buildings, expressways, and shrines all mixed together. Walking down the street I can buy sukiyaki at an exclusive restaurant, or go across the street to Colonel Sanders' Kentucky Fried Chicken. I see Japanese girls in elevator shoes and wearing the layered look, but just behind them is a woman in a kimono, and behind her, an old man with a wispy beard and a cane.

I've never been in a place as intense as Tokyo. Beneath the streets are subways. On the streets are hordes of people. Noise engulfs you. Pollution pushes at you from the sky. Even homes are not a sanctuary from the intensity because if a family buys a 50-foot square lot, they build a home 45 feet square. I decided that my modest suburban split-level home would be a mansion in Tokyo—with enough space for at least six Japanese homes. On the street, skyscrapers along the Ginza reach for the sky—Sony, Nikon, and others. One theatre marquee advertises *The Godfather*, while across the street, *A Streetcar Named Desire* is playing. The next theatre has billboarded *Suburban Wives*. We even export X-rated movies.

Even if you expected the urban side of Tokyo, I'm sure you would be surprised at the champagne flight that lands in Sabah, a country which I first knew as North Borneo. An American school principal who used to live in a hillside home that overlooked the sea had a three-story reinforced concrete school building that compared favorably with schools in American suburbs. I had hoped to meet the president of the Basel Christian Church at the school, but I later met him at the first tee of the Kinabalu Golf Club.

Far away, across the Pacific Ocean and below North America, Latin Americans are fleeing rural poverty and moving into urban chaos. Nineteen Latin American cities have populations of more than one million. By the end of the twentieth century, Mexico City, Sao Paulo, Brazil, Rio de Janiero, and Buenos Aires will be among the ten largest metropolitan areas in the world, each with more than fifteen million residents. Sao Paulo is the fastest growing city in the world. At rush hour it is a human anthill of six million three hundred thousand where Volkswagens clog the streets and sleek buildings shoot upwards. Sao Paulo even has satellite cities—locally known as A, B, C, and D. Each initial stands for a name. A, for example, means Santo Andre. Huge manufacturing plants for Ford, General Motors, Firestone, and Pirelli are located in these satellites.

To the north in Venezuela, the twin towers of the Simon Bolivar Civic Center are a striking centerpiece in downtown Caracas. At lunchtime you can eat a hamburger in one of the shopping centers that mark Nelson Rockefeller's investments in the city. Still further north, the "Mexico miracle" has become a popular phrase. Commercial and business leaders point to new shopping centers, transit systems, factories, and to the country's emergence in 1975 as one of the top ten countries of the world in quantitative economic growth. In 1970, Mexico City had eight million six hundred thousand residents; by 1980, the population will almost have doubled.

Urban Sorespots Too

As glamorous as the new urban world may be, it has not escaped problems common to America. There is traffic congestion, pollution, drug traffic, overpopulation, and the breakdown of family relationships. In Sao Paulo, for example, Waldemir Martin Dias rode thirty hours on a bus from his hometown in northeastern Brazil to find work in the mammoth city. He was hoping to land a job as an unskilled construction worker and then, with luck, to find a factory job. If all went according to plan, Dias said, "He would return to his wife and two children in less than five years, hopefully with enough money to open a small grocery store."

It's not likely to turn out that way, however. Hundreds of rural Brazilians arrive at Sao Paulo's bus terminal every day. At one reception center, migrants are housed and fed free of charge. If after three days they have not found jobs, they must either accept free bus tickets back to their home towns or strike out on their own. If Dias does find a construction job, he will earn about $65 a month—the minimum wage. He will end up living in one of the squatters settlements in the city, or in one-room tenements with no running water or sanitary facilities. By 1990, two out of three Latin Americans may be living in urban areas, and the vast majority of these city residents will be dwelling in slums or other sub-standard housing. The Latin American situation only emphasizes the "coming Third World crisis" predicted by some sociologists —the runaway growth in the large cities.

Coinciding with the population crunch is the problem of pollution. A 1975 Gallup Poll reported that 82 percent of the population of Greater Sao Paulo considered air pollution there "very serious." 82 percent said that smoke from factories and industry was the main cause of the city's air pollution, while 55 percent held "the excessive number of vehicles, buses, and cars" responsible. During an atmospheric inversion, one suburb reported a record rate of air pollution of 54.9 percent—that is, the percentage of polluted air to pure air. The air was thick, white, and acrid-smelling with layers of smoke and dust. Residents complained of sore throats and smarting eyes.

In urban Singapore, "long hair and drug abuse are part of the drug subculture found in Asian countries," says John Hanam of the Singapore Central Narcotics Bureau. "However, long hair is but one symbol associated with drugs. There are other trappings like patched pants, leather collars, and leather watch straps which are worn by some university students. If symbols like these are done away with, then interest in drugs will also be stepped down." Several years ago, former Pennsylvania Governor Raymond P. Shafer, then chairman of the U. S. Commission on Marijuana and Drug Abuse, went to Singapore to study a police crackdown on drug use among the young. He found that newspapers gave large headlines to official admonitions about hippies, drugs, draft dodgers, unethical teachers, long hair, water waste, sloppy dress, and littering.

Family breakdown has found its place in the overseas urban life. Divorce is more frequent in India as women increasingly assert their rights. Rama Chander, a thirty-one-year-old secretary in a modern office in New Delhi, says that she "never would have thought of divorce five years ago. I would have suffered through an unhappy marriage until I died. But I heard of other women who were divorced, and that gave me the strength to try." In Bombay, about one thousand divorces were recorded in 1975, three times as many as eight years earlier. A Calcutta woman said that she "now has proper dates with men from the place where I work, and I no longer rule out the possibility that I may someday be someone's wife again."

In Malaysia and Singapore, Chinese youth are not as self-disciplined as their parents, and they want more liberties than their elders enjoyed when they were young. "Times have changed," the youth say, but their parents fail to agree. Young people quarrel with their parents over standards of morality. "Why should I go to church?" they ask. "If I don't steal or kill, I'm O.K. The important thing is to get your own pleasure and not quarrel with others."

On a still deeper level, the problems of the urban world—accentuated by over-populated cities—means that some totalitarian governments have taken strict measures which hamper human freedoms. In India, intellectuals express caution, fear, and concern about their future in a country where the constitutional powers are in flux. Contributors to intellectual magazines are not willing to write the bold things they want to publish. Film makers steer clear of the biting social realism that characterized former films because, in the words of a Calcutta filmmaker, "This is not the time to make sharp comments on political subjects." On another front, India sterilized some five million people during an eight-month period in 1976. The sterilizations are part of a sweeping government birth control campaign which is aimed at curbing the country's population increase of one million per month.

In other countries, repression uses different means. The pleas of blacks for justice in Namibia and Rhodesia are well documented. Amnesty International, a London-based human rights organization, says that more than sixty of the world's one hundred and forty countries are practicing systematic torture of their political prisoners. In Iran, for example, the secret police uses such torture techniques as flogging, electrical shocks, tearing out fingernails and toenails, rape, and genital torture.

Not Four Worlds But One

All these things—and more—are part of the world which is now our home. The shrinking globe, the rapidity of communications, the incessant growth of cities and the problems that confront them, and the multinational corporations which throw an economic net over the world are the marks of the emerging global village. To make matters more manageable, some authorities have divided our new world into four sections. The First World is made up of the industrial democracies, mostly in the West—nations such as Australia, Canada, Denmark, Japan, the

Netherlands, South Africa, the United Kingdom, the United States, and West Germany.

The Second World is made up of the communist states, such as Albania, China, Cuba, East Germany, North Korea, Vietnam, and Russia. The Third World is comprised of the developing nations, including countries such as Brazil, Equador, Egypt, Ghana, Liberia, Nigeria, New Guinea, Philippines, Saudi Arabia, Singapore, Tunisia, and Venezuela. The Fourth World is a listing of the most economically disadvantaged countries such as Bangladesh, Burundi, Haiti, India, Malawai, the Sudan, Uganda, and Western Samoa.

But whenever such divisions are made, we must remember that our planet is not made up of four worlds but of one world. John Donne reminded us many years ago that "No man is an island." He was right. No one lives in isolation. As an individual person, we long for companionship. As a family, we rely upon the network of schools, hospitals, stores, and community services to make our lives more pleasant. Deep down inside ourselves we know that we can never develop fully as human beings apart from other people.

The same is also true of countries. No nation today is an island unto itself. National independence is no longer possible for any nation without world interdependence. Independence might bring the excitement of attempting to achieve things on our own, but the world has arrived at a stage where no nation can afford to be concerned only for itself. Getting a glimpse of the rest of this planet as our home can help us understand what it means to be a world citizen, to learn of the strengths of other cultures, to be thankful for what we have, and perhaps to view our country from outside and even come to understand—if not to appreciate—why some of the things are said about us abroad. To acquire a vision of the world as our home is a little like getting a vision of the hereafter. Once you do, your present horizon will never be the same.

Indian and American pastors dedicate village church

2 Declaring Interdependence

The year was 1968, and the place was Asmara, Ethiopia. President Sueaki Utsumi of the Japan Evangelical Lutheran Church was attending a conference of the Lutheran World Federation. There, 8,000 miles from the slopes of Mount Fuji—without either the knowledge or approval of the Japan church's executive committee—President Utsumi declared to Lutherans in the rest of the world that the Japan Evangelical Lutheran Church would be self-supporting by the end of 1974.

The Lutheran World Federation cheered the statement but that same statement was also greeted by jeers when Utsumi returned to Japan. Some older leaders, accustomed to the comfortable support of overseas Lutherans, were openly critical of Utsumi. Others, many of them younger pastors, eager to see Japan fulfill its destiny as a church and as a nation, said, "It's about time."

No one in the history of Lutheran missions had ever made a statement like Utsumi before—let alone putting a date to it. And yet, that very declaration was the kind of fulfillment that American missionaries and Japanese Lutherans had dreamed about for years. The "daughter" was cutting herself away from the "mother" and striking out on her own. Lutherans have been at work in Japan since 1893, with congregations usually receiving both their property and church building from overseas. In many cases, the pastor's salary was paid from abroad whether the pastor was Japanese or a missionary. Many congregations were so accustomed to overseas support that they averaged twenty-eight years in becoming self-supporting.

Between 1968 and 1975—the target date for self-reliance—the Japan Evangelical Lutheran Church worked hard to fulfill its promise. It had sufficient pastors but financial considerations were another matter. Only seventy-one of the JELC's one hundred and forty-five congregations were self-supporting by 1975. Per capita giving by the sixteen thousand members of the church was about $100 a year. To meet its goal, the leaders of the JELC decided that a congregation of forty active members would be expected to become self-supporting, and that congregations needed to increase their benevolence contributions from about 11 percent of their income to 40 percent.

In addition to congregations paying their own expenses, stronger congregations were expected to provide funds to subsidize weaker churches. In the Kyushu district in southern Japan, for example, the twenty-five self-supporting congregations were asked to supply sufficient funds to help operate the twenty-nine other congregations in the district. New mission congregations were to be started largely through the combined efforts of the district and the church's central administration augmented occasionally by overseas aid. Moreover, the homes for children and the aging, and the boys' and girls' high schools in Kumamoto were expected to become financially independent.

On January 1, 1975, the Japan Evangelical Lutheran Church's promise became a reality. Funds from the Lutheran Church in America which had been used to underwrite the central administration of the JELC, its congregations, and pastors was stopped. Overseas missionaries continued their work in Japan only at the invitation of the JELC. Lutherans in America continued to supply financial aid to expensive, on-going projects such as the seminary, but all decisions were made jointly.

The new direction of the Japan Evangelical Lutheran Church and the new mission strategy required by its American partner are being repeated over and over in various parts of the world. In plain terms, the "era of interdependence" has come to world missions. The term has a warm, wholesome ring. It fits in well with the concept of the world as our home. But for many Americans it is a challenge, because independence—rather than interdependence—has been our watchword. Shifting one's mental gears in such a way is imperative in thinking about the overseas relationships of the church in a world that is becoming increasingly sophisticated, educated, industrialized, Westernized, nationalistic, and urban.

Against this background, American churches have been overhauling their mission philosophies radically. The Board of International Ministries of the American Baptist Churches in the U.S.A. now says:

"We have entered a period when mission is no longer exclusively the outreach from the developed Western churches to proclaim the Gospel to unevangelized peoples and develop indigenous churches. Today churches throughout the world have become mature partners, both sending and receiving the Christian witness in many forms of international exchange. This is also a time when the more affluent churches of the West are discovering that they need to be renewed by the fresh Christian witness of churches of other nations."

In its report on Latin America for 1975, the Division of International Mission of the Presbyterian Church in the U.S. says:

"Evangelizing and establishing new churches, bringing them to self-support and moving on to new areas is no longer a theory but a reality. Areas comparable in size and eventually to be two presbyteries, where work began ten to twelve years earlier, is now totally out of mission hands and the final subsidies for this work are fast coming to a close."

Robert A. Thomas, chairman of the Division of Overseas Ministries of the Christian Church (Disciples of Christ), says, "We must learn to transfer loyalties and concern from *our* missionaries to Christ's mission, and that is most difficult."

Other architects of updated mission philosophy have

referred to the various "stages" of mission work. For example, David M. Stowe, executive Vice President of the United Church of Christ Board for World Ministries, says that mission has gone through three stages:

"The first missionaries were planters. They went out to far places in the world to proclaim the faith, gather a community of believers and establish the church. That stage is over. We do not send 'planters' anymore. The seed has been planted; the church has been established in nearly every country.

"Next, missionaries were managers, operating institutions such as hospitals, schools, and church structures. That stage is nearly over. We have only a few persons managing anything overseas today. Leaders of indigenous churches are the managers of their own institutions. They do not want personnel from abroad to manage what they are determined to manage for themselves. They want freedom to develop their own institutions to fit their own needs on the basis of their own understanding of the Gospel and the work of the church.

"If there is no longer need for planters and managers, what is left? Servanthood. The only shape of mission acceptable in the Third World is the servant role. And the only persons who should be sent overseas today are those capable of servanthood; those who can enable action to liberate, to humanize, to change structures and systems; those who can work on behalf of the partnership between churches here and churches there without attempting to manage. Such persons are in demand everywhere in the world. Nobody wants *them* to 'go home.'"

David Vikner, executive director of the Division for World Mission and Ecumenism of the Lutheran Church in America, says that stage one of mission activity dates from the beginning of the missionary movement up until about 1945. During this time, Lutherans sent missionaries to such places as Japan, China, Tanzania, Liberia, Argentina, and Guyana. Mission success was measured by the number of missionaries sent, and the number of fields occupied. Mission societies came into being to support missionaries and mission executives as they "carved up" much of the world to avoid duplication of efforts. In Southeast Asia for example, the Methodists evangelized Malaya. Presbyterians were sent to Thailand, Baptists were in Burma, the Christian Missionary Alliance went to Vietnam, and the Lutherans and the Reformed Churches concentrated on Indonesia.

Then, says Vikner, came stage two, which dates generally from 1945 to 1970. In these years, the overseas churches became somewhat autonomous, electing their own leaders and staffing their congregations with their own pastors. But they were heavily subsidized by U.S. Lutherans and others to cover the cost of their central administration, purchase of land, and the erection of buildings. The focus at this stage was to have the overseas church serve as the channel for support from outside agencies. This was a sort of transition period when the United States was still making most of the decisions.

Now, Vikner continues, we have come to stage three—the period from 1970 to the present. If stage two was the beginning of the independent era of overseas churches, stage three is the era of interdependence. This third stage takes into account the national assertiveness of overseas countries—their determination to do things themselves with self-respect and self-identity. It recognizes that modernization has reached every country in one form or another. It takes note of the decline in American influence in many countries. It recognizes that the overseas churches have gained maturity and confidence, and have become increasingly vocal in expressing their views about their treatment at the hands of the older churches. Various indigenous forms of worship have been adopted, along with theologies and organizational structures which fit their cultural settings. The Lutheran Church in America has even gone so far as to set a time line when various overseas churches are to become self-reliant. Japan was the first in 1975. Tanzania is scheduled for self-reliance in the late seventies, with Hong Kong, Malaysia, Guyana, and India slated for 1980. Liberia is due for self-reliance in 1982.

The shift is from "parent" to "partner." In more philosophic terms, the declaration of interdependence between the mission efforts of churches in North America and the churches of the rest of the world is described by the Lutheran Church in America as "independent, autonomous, self-reliant partners interdependently sharing their resources to carry out the mission committed to them by their Lord."

Missionary Go Home

The rapidly changing nature of the world is not the only reason for a change in mission philosophy. Outright antagonism from some parts of the world, such as Africa, has resulted in a request for a moratorium on all missionaries *and* funds from American churches. At the Third Assembly of the All Africa Conference of Churches in Lusaka, Zambia in May 1974, such a moratorium was requested. John Gatu of Kenya, chairman of the AACC General Committee said,

"We cannot build the church in Africa on alms given by overseas churches nor are we serving the cause of the kingdom by turning all bishops, general secretaries, moderators, and presidents into 'good ecclesiastical beggars' by always singing the tune of poverty in the churches of the Third World."

The AACC proposed four reasons why a moratorium would be desirable:

1. To discover an authentic African form of Christianity which can in turn enrich all the Christian churches of the world;

2. To encourage African churches to leave the dependent attitudes many have adopted;

3. To help African churches to establish their own priorities in their work for Christ and to become fully missionary churches themselves;

4. To enable the traditionally missionary-sending churches in other lands to reexamine the nature of their mission and their future partnership with other churches.

The African Christians recognized that the moratorium would force them to take full responsibility for the work of their church and to support it completely. But leaders also pointed out that similar conditions had been forced on churches in the past. During World War I, Lutheran missionaries in the Usambara Mountains of Tanzania and Presbyterian missionaries in what is now Togo and Ghana had to leave their churches there. Missionaries of the Sudan Interior Mission had to leave their churches in Ethiopia during the Italian invasion prior to World War II. These churches, leaders pointed out, not only survived such enforced moratoriums, but were strengthened by discovering their won self-reliance. They also pointed out that a number of independent churches have grown up in Africa in recent years which have not had relationships with churches overseas. One example is the "Kimbanguist" Church of Zaire which developed in this way to its present membership of four million. In the last three years, though, the idea of moratorium has been generally acknowledged as an emphasis on allowing overseas churches to set their own direction. Most mission officials and churches around the world agree that independence was not the goal but rather an enlightened sense of interdependence.

Aside from the moratorium issue, national independence in many countries brought about the need for rethinking American involvement overseas. Some countries restrict teachers as missionaries but allow evangelistic missionaries (Japan). Others restrict evangelistic missionaries and allow teachers (India). Malaysia has put a ten-year limit upon a missionary's presence. After that time, a missionary may be replaced, but no one can spend an entire missionary career in that country. One analysis suggests that missionaries are prohibited from reaching nearly two billion people in countries such as China, Russia, and Eastern Europe where political considerations are major factors.

There is also torture of missionaries. In late 1976, two Roman Catholic priests were deported from the Philippines and a Maryknoll sister was denied a visa extension. During 1976, a Roman Catholic bishop was sentenced to ten years in prison in Rhodesia; two priests were shot and a bishop beaten in Brazil; eighteen Christians, including several clergy, were given stiff prison sentences in South Korea; several missionaries were arrested in Paraguay; fifteen bishops, including four from the United States, and twenty-two priests were expelled from Ecuador; seven priests, two seminarians, and three nuns were shot in Argentina by right-wing groups which have been linked to the police.

Another example of nationalistic inhospitality toward missionaries is expressed in a report from the All Africa Conference of Churches which says, "the Christian press has no future in Uganda." According to the news bureau, the death in 1976 of the editor of the Roman Catholic daily newspaper *Munno* resulted from the newspaper's printing of an article which allegedly "incited sedition" to the rule of Idi Amin. Under the military regime of Amin, several journalists have "disappeared." The late Father Clement Kiggundi, a former editor of *Munno*, was taken away by Amin's soldiers and was not seen alive thereafter. The editor's remains were later found burned in his car a few miles outside Kampala. The newspaper has now been closed under government orders.

Another indication of the practical necessity for interdependence in the mission efforts of American churches and their overseas counterparts is the continuing uncertainty about the role of the West in these countries. I have often heard university students question the role of the West. One student named Vani at the Women's Christian College in Madras said, "Five years ago, we would have been more friendly toward the United States. But we have to be so careful with your country. You don't assure us of continual help." Another woman student said, "The United States has been putting its finger into countries all over the world, and that hasn't always been good for the country involved. We don't want that to happen here. We don't want India to become dependent on the U.S., or for the U.S. to have a 'hold' on us."

A young Indian pastor, Prabhakara Rao, noted that "sometimes the United States assistance causes our pastors to have problems. Non-Christians claim the pastors are fed by Americans and that the pastors therefore preach the American gospel—that Christianity is a foreign religion."

In Japan, Yojiro Mishima, a freshman at Hosei University who is studying electrical engineering, told me that "America is not a close friend of ours. America as a Christian country has killed people in Vietnam and Cambodia. We have trouble understanding that." Another student, Akazawa Shinya, a senior in economics in Keio University in Tokyo, said that "Up to now, Japan has had closer relations with America than with any other country. But now we should start having closer relations with countries near to Japan. We can have better relations with China than with the U.S.," he said.

Encouraging Results

When these practical and political realities are added to the sociological shifts now under way in overseas society, the church missions' "era of interdependence" comes into sharper focus. Many questions are answered, and even those who are skeptical of self-reliance find that their fears can be allayed. Doing things themselves is really what overseas Christians want. The congregation of Osaka Lutheran Church in Japan, for example, has torn down its small church which was located near an express-way exit ramp and a subway station. The congregation has built an eight-story hotel with nearly two hundred rooms, and has placed the church's sanctuary on the top floor. The hotel rooms are providing the Japan Evangelical Lutheran Church more than $40,000 a year to aid the support of the central administration of the church and the development of new congregations. Even more exciting is the boldness of the forty-three-member Sendai Lutheran Church 200 miles north of Tokyo. The congregation itself is not yet self-supporting, but it accepted a $200,000 challenge to build a day care center in its community. The pastor of the congregation discussed the matter with the district officers of the JELC and the churches of the district decided to pool their resources to finance "their" project. Today, the day care center serves ninety youngsters and will also be the home of another Lutheran church.

Christian leaders in Japan, as well as in other parts of the world, are careful to point out that self-reliance does not mean independence. They recognize that politically, some countries say, "Yankee go home." But church leaders do not wish for missionaries to leave their countries entirely. Bishop Josiah Kibira of the Evangelical Lutheran Church in Tanzania says that "There is hardly any foreign mission which acts by itself in any part of the world." He feels that mission agencies must "help each other reciprocally preach the gospel" in different lands. Like others, Bishop Kibira cautions that no church can be fully "self-reliant" without damaging desirable interchurch cooperation. Hence, the emphasis on interdependence.

The strategy is analogous to that which occurred at the time of the Revolution in the United States in 1776. The thirteen newly independent American states soon found that independence was not exactly what they wanted. Their political and economic fortunes were interlinked. They lacked the capacity to manage their economic and trade problems and to maintain peace and security in isolation from each other. The wise and innovative leadership of George Washington, Benjamin Franklin, James Madison, and Alexander Hamilton helped the states face up to the fact that more than independence was required to assure a viable society. This set in motion the drafting of the Constitution of the United States, which, in 1788, was adopted by the delegates from the politically independent states to form the interdependence of the United States.

The interdependent role of American mission efforts in the future seems clear. Denomination after denomination is adopting the view that "independent, autonomous, self-reliant partners will interdependently share their resources to carry out the mission committed to them by their Lord." Some questions remain—and will be dealt with later in this book. For example, in the "era of interdependence," how many American missionaries can be sent overseas and what will they do? What can be said about the gospel imperative to "Go into all the world . . ." if some cultures are unfriendly? What will be the shape and growth of the church around the world in the future? Hint: The Christian church is now growing more rapidly in virtually every part of the world than in western Europe or the United States, the major missionary-sending countries of the past.

3 The Ecumenical Emphasis

When Ronald and Edith Seaton were jointly appointed as public health missionaries to India by three protestant denominations, church mission history was made. Their appointment marked the first time that the United Presbyterian Church, the United Church of Christ, and the Christian Church (Disciples of Christ) joined together in making a missionary appointment. David M. Stowe, executive vice president of the United Church Board for World Ministries, told the Seatons, "You are sent by three boards which are growing toward unity. We pledge our united love to you."

In the tiny Himalayan country of Nepal just north of India, Neil Solvik made another kind of ecumenical mission history. Not only was Solvik the first missionary sent by the Lutheran Church in America to Nepal, he also represented that thurch's first involvement with the United Mission to Nepal, an ecumenical mission agency which represents twenty-nine mission societies and countries from more than a dozen countries. The United Mission to Nepal is one of few Christian organizations allowed in Nepal. All of them operate under special permission of King Birendra and His Majesty's Government.

Another kind of ecumenical organization, the All Africa Conference of Churches, has linked traditional faith with the movements for independence in a manner that has given it a level of influence unmatched by any other regional ecumenical body. It acted effectively in helping settle civil wars in Sudan and Nigeria, and has been closely identified with forces fighting white governments in southern Africa. It has also provided basic services to thousands of political refugees. Because it is ecumenical in nature, the conference is able to exert strong social and political influence on the continent.

The rapidly advancing ecumenical nature of missions may surprise some Americans. But that surprise is likely caused by the fact that Christianity has always been a majority religion in North America. By contrast, 3 percent of the population of Malaysia and Singapore is Christian. In neighboring Japan, only 1 percent of the population is Christian. These statistics need to be taken to heart. When Christians make up only 3 percent of the population of a country—or 1 percent—they must work together if the church is to have any impact on local affairs. Simply being Christian is being distinctive in Malaysia, Singapore, and Japan—and causes distinctions between being Methodist or Lutheran or Baptist to pale into relative insignificance.

The mission policy of most churches is recognizing the ecumenical imperative. Robert A. Thomas, chairman of the Division of Overseas Ministries of the Christian Church (Disciples of Christ) says, "We are engaged in scarcely any work overseas that is strictly denominational, and that only because there are no ecumenical organizations to which to relate. We work with union churches in Japan, the Philippines, Hong Kong, Indonesia, India, Okinawa, Thailand, Zaire, Zambia, and Brazil. We are encouraging negotiations on church union in South Africa, Jamaica, and several Latin American countries."

The Division of International Missions of the Presbyterian Church in the U.S. reports that sixty-eight of its missionaries in Asia and the South Pacific are working in partnership with the missionaries from the Presbyterian Church of Korea, the United Presbyterian Church in the U.S.A., and the Australian Presbyterian Church. In similar manner, a study by the American Baptist Churches in the U.S.A. in 1975 revealed that 20 percent of its overseas missionary force was working in cooperative endeavors ranging from major medical centers to councils of churches, from universities to hostels for missionaries' children, from Bible translation to the distribution of Christian literature, from evangelistic programs to community development projects.

David Vikner, executive director of the Division for World Mission and Ecumenism of the Lutheran Church in America, has committed his church to one of the strongest ecumenical statements: "We should not seek to plant the Lutheran Church in new areas of the world, but should, rather, cooperate with any and all Christian groups existing in the area which are engaged in the mission of Christ, be they Lutheran, Roman Catholic, ecumenical, conservative evangelical, or Pentecostal." He explains that the Lutheran Church in America takes seriously the biblical imperative "that they may all be one." In practical terms, he adds, "the needs of the world require more resources of information, manpower, and money than the entire church, much less any single denomination, possesses."

Cooperative Seminaries

Certainly one of the most striking examples of ecumenical effort is in theological education. Americans do not generally agree that pastors should be trained at interdenominational seminaries; we prefer for each church to train its own leaders. Overseas, however, ecumenical seminaries are commonplace. Trinity Theological College in Singapore trains ministerial students from all parts of southeastern Asia, be they Anglican, Lutheran, Presbyterian, or Methodist. "When you come here, you become newly aware of what it means to be a Lutheran," said one student from Kuala Lumpur. "But because we have been here, we'll be better able to work with other Christians later."

Trinity College was founded in 1948. Today, the majority of students are Methodists while most of the faculty are Presbyterians. "You'd be surprised at how easily such cooperation works," says a professor from the Church of

Sweden. "We have different systems of thinking about theology, but we find that at the bottom of the matter we are much the same. We act as people in society, and there is where each of us is Christian."

In 1964, Andhra Christian Theological College was established in India by uniting the previous seminaries of the Lutheran church, the Baptist church, and the Church of South India. A few years later, the Methodist Church of Southern Asia joined the college also.

"Each of the participating denominations has its own 'hall'," explains William Coleman, dean of the college. "There are two hours of instruction each week about the liturgy, history, and polity of each denomination," he says. "Each hall also has its special day each year (like Reformation Day for the Lutherans) in which everyone participates."

Another school in India which prepares pastors is the United Theological College in Bangalore which has relationships with twenty-one mission societies. William P. Peery, a Lutheran professor of systematic theology, says that the ecumenical approach makes sense because "the church in India long ago realized that the denominational accidents of religious history in Europe and America had little consequence for India. Even the matter of Luther and the Roman Catholic Church was not of great consequence to the Indian mind. The challenge from non-Christians became pointed—what type of Christian should I become?"

Russell Chandran, principal of the United Theological College, says that the seminary "leads the Indian church in articulating its own faith in freedom from the molds of western Christianity but without rejecting the heritage of the western church. The Indian church must regard the faith and heritage of India as its contribution to the ecumenical movement." Then Chandran laughed. "Did you know that when we send teachers to America for education, they stay there because of the increased teaching opportunity they find for courses on eastern religions? We've lost at least a

half-dozen men this way in the last ten years. And some U.S. seminary presidents have talked to me about their children who have gone off to study eastern religions!"

In the western hemisphere, the United Church of Christ helps support the Latin American Biblical Seminary in San Jose, Costa Rica, where liberation theology and the charismatic movement coexist. The one hundred and thirty students enrolled in the seminary come from seventeen Latin American countries and represent forty-two Christian denominations. Not far away at the United Theological College of the West Indies in Kingston, Jamaica, Sheldon Dewsbury, a Baptist from Trinidad, took his training with eighty students, of whom nineteen were Methodist, sixteen Baptist, fifteen Moravian, fifteen Anglican, nine Presbyterian, six Lutheran, and two from the United Church of Jamaica and Grand Cayman.

The experiences of ecumenical theological education are only a glimpse of the range of cooperative activities. Let me broaden the scope:

Liberia. A joint Christian education curriculum has been designed by the Lutheran and Methodist churches. This curriculum is written by Liberians for Liberians and published jointly by the two churches. A television project titled "Concern" is produced jointly, and the two denominations operate a book store and audio-visual film library.

Tanzania. One project of the Christian Council of Tanzania is urban missions—with Lutheran and Anglican staff workers and a governing board headed by a Roman Catholic. The council sponsors an ecumenical Christmas pageant in the national stadium in Dar es Salaam, and a joint Easter procession that gathers participants from each church en route to a city park. Lutherans, Anglicans, and Moravians have developed a common liturgy and are working on a joint hymnal.

Sabah. In Kota Kinabalu, capital of the state of Sabah, the president of the Basel Christian Church's high school is

Wong Fook Kui, a Buddhist. At a similar church school in Sandakan, the president is Peter Cheng, a Roman Catholic. His assistant is Mohammad Zain, a Muslim.

Ghana. A missionary of the Lutheran Church in America works with the "Good News Institute" to deepen the biblical and theological undergirding of leaders of the independent, indigenous, Pentecostal-type churches that are growing at a rapid rate in African Christianity. An ecumenical program, "Islam in Africa," helps Christians develop a sympathetic understanding of Muslim beliefs, biases, and taboos, thereby aiding them to present the gospel in a way that is winsome rather than repulsive.

Singapore. In designing Jurong Industrial Estate, a 17,000-acre high-rise apartment and manufacturing complex, the government of Singapore allotted one "religious" site for the building of a church. When it was awarded to the Lutherans, the denomination erected a $165,000 church and civic center but named it simply "Jurong Christian Center." The use of the word *Christian* is deliberate. Since the church is the only one on the estate, candidates for baptism are instructed in the Lutheran faith but members of fourteen other churches have become "affiliate" members without officially changing their previous denominational alliances. The staff is interdenominational, often including Lutheran, Methodist, and Anglican clergy.

Philippines. Eunice Runes was an outstanding student at Ellinwood College of Christian Education in 1969. She went to the United States to seminary and there married a seminarian. Their return to the Philippines, however, proved to be a cooperative venture. The United Board for Higher Education in Asia arranged their transportation, Joel Runes' salary was paid by the Christian Church (Disciples of Christ) and the United Presbyterian Church, and the couple's housing was provided by the Philippine Christian College where she is a teacher and he is a chaplain.

India. One-third of the two million eight hundred thousand residents of Madras lives in dried palm-leaf "temporary" houses tucked alongside bridges and jammed into small open spaces. The government is trying to clear the slums, but in the meantime, some joint efforts by Lutherans, the Church of South India, the Mar Thoma Church, a Methodist woman and some non-Christians are making life a little easier for these people. Viji Srinivasan is a petite, energetic Brahmin who talks proudly about the twenty-five day care centers she has helped establish, and the high food-value baby food mixture which she makes available to the mothers. Dorothy Leith, a Methodist from England, helped form the Madras Christian Service Center which operates a job placement service, study courses and training for community leaders, and residential care for young people who are preparing to be social workers. The center brought together Leith and Srinivasan in a program known as "Happy Homes" which trains social workers to teach young mothers child care, family budgeting, first aid, road safety, nutrition, and how to cope with alcoholism.

Church Mergers

Not all ecumenical emphasis occurs at the local level. In 1947, the Church of South India came into being through a merger of the mission efforts of the Anglican, Congregational, Presbyterian, Methodist, and Reformed churches. At present, five different Lutheran churches in the same part of the country are considering merger with the CSI. The new church might be called the "Church of Christ in South India."

But church mergers move slowly in any country. Samuel W. Schmitthenner, president of the Andhra Evangelical Lutheran Church, the largest Lutheran group in the country, says that "as a responsible Christian leader, I have to work toward church union. But as a missionary, I feel that I cannot push the church in a direction that its people and pastors do not want. So I'm taking the long view of trying to reeducate the clergy and laity."

The executive council of the Andhra Evangelical Lutheran Church has authorized altar and pulpit fellowship with the Church of South India. The Lutherans work together in seminaries, publications, and other institutions. Many younger pastors are anxious to bring about the merger.

Bishop Sundar Clarke of the Madras diocese of the Church of South India has sharp words about the Lutheran hesitance. The bishop sipped a Fanta orange drink as he talked in his office on the cathedral compound. "In the Church of South India, we are very eager for union with the Lutherans," he said. "Theologically, there is nothing to divide us. Liturgically there is very little to keep us apart. The Lutheran liturgy would enrich us. It's the non-doctrinal items which keep us separate, mostly items of vested interest, property, and prestige."

"The Lutheran leaders also seemed to come up with non-theological excuses about union," the bishop continued. One man said, "Our leader would lose his chance to go to America if we merged. If you ask me when Lutherans will join the Church of South India, I would answer, when American dollars stop coming to India."

"Lutherans also seem to fear that they will be swallowed up and lose their tradition if they come into the Church of South India," the bishop continued. "But if Lutherans come into the Church of South India we will lose our tradition too. If our particularities are lost, however, it is for the greater gain of coming together." The bishop recalled that the Methodists, Presbyterians, and Congregationalists feared that, after 1947, the Church of South India would become an "Anglican affair" because of the emphasis on the episcopacy. But those fears did not materialize. The bishop admitted, however, that the Church of South India could learn a little from the Lutherans about respect for tradition.

"In the Church of South India, there is no real holding on to tradition," he said. "Those who came together were predisposed to forget the past."

The purpose of these ecumenical efforts—whether cooperative seminary training or joint ministry to human need—is to proclaim the oneness of Christ through a united witness in his church. But the practical side is also apparent. For example, Christian councils of churches play a more dominant role overseas than in the United States. These councils can command resources that individual churches cannot. Individual churches can draw only upon the resources of the mission agencies of their churches.

The councils also have more clout with the local government. When India cracked down on granting visas a few years ago, those churches whose negotiations were handled through the National Council of Churches in India fared much better than mission boards that negotiated with the government alone.

It is also desirable that overseas churches relate to more than one church in North America. In Tanzania, for example, sixteen American and European mission agencies assist the program and personnel needs of the Evangelical Lutheran Church of Tanzania. This process, which is sometimes termed "multinational," reflects both the ecumenical nature of the church and good world strategy. When several outside agencies support an overseas church, the cultural overlays which missionaries have so often been accused of instilling are not so predominant.

One final message of this ecumenical emphasis is that the overseas experience may have some influence upon the less ecumenically-minded churches in North America. Some of the twenty-nine mission agencies which cooperate in the United Mission to Nepal, for instance, are officially antiecumenical and would not have anything to do with some of the UMN churches in their home countries. But because the government restriction in Nepal prevents churches from individually sending missionaries, these "antiecumenical" churches cooperate in that Himalayan country. It is ironic that many mission-minded churches find cooperation more easily accomplished abroad than at home. Whether this ecumenical experience overseas will bring further unanimity among the churches on the home front remains to be seen.

4 Lay People Are the Key

The road to Namo Ukur is narrow and bumpy. It starts out paved, and then becomes a dirt road. On either side is the tangled undergrowth typical of northern Indonesia. Then a church with split bamboo walls and a palm-thatched roof stands in a clearing amid a few houses and farmlands.

"One thousand people will be baptized here next month," a heavily tanned chief of police of Namo Ukur told me. He is the elder of the congregation, and even though a pastor occasionally visits them, the police chief is the spiritual leader in the community. As such, he is following a pattern brought to northern Sumatra by Ludwig I. Nommensen in 1862. Nommensen enlisted the help of village chiefs to enhance the peoples' receptivity to the gospel.

In addition to his leadership in the Namo Ukur congregation, the police chief, with the musical name of S. Sembiring, is also an evangelist. He contacts leaders in nearby villages asking for permission to conduct evangelistic services. Sembiring walks fourteen miles several nights a week to conduct a meeting which starts at 10 P.M. He does not get home until 3 A.M.

"Sometimes I spend so much time with the church that I get behind on my police work," he says, "but then the crime rate has been going down since people became Christian. There's less stealing and gambling." Village chiefs welcome Sembiring and ask their townspeople to listen to him. Sembiring prays, preaches, leads singing, and answers questions.

Church leaders like Sembiring are one-half of the reason why "lay people are the key" in overseas missions today.

Indonesians are the best evangelists for Indonesians, just as Africans are the best evangelists for Africans, and Brazilians are the best evangelists for Brazilians. Sembiring gets assistance in his preaching duties when Indonesian Pastor P. Bukit, who serves nineteen congregations besides the Namo Ukur parish, gathers the elders from the twenty congregations each week to help them prepare a sermon which they deliver in their congregations the following Sunday.

The other half of the reason that "lay people are the key" is that most North American churches are sending far more lay people overseas than clergy. Only 35 percent of the missionaries of the Lutheran Church in America, for example, are clergy. Most of the overseas churches are supplying their own pastors. In Japan, no American is serving as senior pastor of a Lutheran congregation; the only American pastors in that country are serving as associate pastors. Consequently, North American churches are sending to the overseas churches lay specialists such as hospital administrators, urban planners, pharmacists, agriculturalists, curriculum writers, radio technicians, and business managers to help fill particular needs and to train indigenous leaders to take over the jobs. Most of these lay missionaries are short-term missionaries, spending two or three years in a country and then returning to North America to continue their regular careers.

In like manner, only one-third of the one hundred and eighty-six missionaries of the United Church of Christ are actively engaged in evangelism among persons of other faiths and ideologies. Another one-third are "evangelists once-removed," that is, working in specialized jobs with persons who are already Christian.

Some stories of these lay evangelists are fascinating. When the Sudan Interior Mission entered southern Ethiopia in the early 1930's, it made contact with three members of the Kembatta tribe. Severo Wosoro, Shugate Dada, and Abagoli Worsoro were converted to Christianity, but before the missionaries could reach large numbers of people, the Italians invaded Ethiopia and the missionaries were forced to leave the country.

These three men were literate, so they started a school and taught people to read the Bible. Before long, Abagoli became such a zealous evangelist that he was arrested and jailed by the Italians. After questioning, they let him go, deciding that such a barely literate fellow was too ignorant to cause any trouble. But when the missionaries of the Sudan Interior Mission returned to Ethiopia, they discovered fifty thousand converts who could be traced to the work of these three men. The Kembatta synod is now part of the Mekane Yesus Church (Lutheran).

Thousands of miles away in the Indian village of Amruthalur, the sounds coming from the Hindu temple grounds were quite unusual. There were songs, dances, and testimony about the Christian gospel. Some of the speakers stood where Hindu priests would normally stand. B. V. Subbamma could hardly believe the size of the crowd. Christians would usually not even walk in front of the temple, and Hindus had to have a ceremonial bath to be there. But the temple grounds were filled with more than two thousand people.

Two hours later, some hundred people were still waiting to talk with Subbamma and her colleagues. Many told her they had been thinking of becoming Christians for years, but were afraid to make the break with their family or their culture. Subbamma took their names and turned them over to Christians in the community who had been invited to the service. At a similar gathering a year before, a number of Hindus had been baptized, including the wife of the headmaster of the local school.

This scene is being repeated in hundreds of communities as part of the most significant evangelism movement in Indian Lutheranism today. The movement's leader, a lay woman named B. V. Subbamma, is one of the country's most exciting evangelists. Christians have generally made their largest gains in India by baptizing outcaste people from the lowest rung of Indian society. For them, the gospel means hope—a quality of life which has virtually eluded them since they normally can find only menial jobs and are forced to live in certain sections of the city.

But Subbamma is a member of the Sudhra artisan caste, and knows how to attract caste people. Her major technique is scheduling mass gatherings in Hindu sections of towns. There, women trained by Subbamma sing Bible-story lyrics set to the music of Hindu folk tunes and present dramas such as the Good Samaritan. Her work involves the sponsoring of ashrams, retreats where Christians share the gospel with Hindus. It also means the eventual establishment of Sudhra congregations in members' homes because these caste Christians won't go to church in the outcaste ghettos of a town.

Subbamma became familiar with ashrams, because of her Hindu background where they are used for fellowship, sharing of burdens, meditation, and study. Subbamma's first ashram attracted one hundred and eighty-three women, both newly baptized Christians and Hindus interested in the gospel. The following year, four hundred people were present, including some men. "In many cases, husbands won't let their wives go to church," Subbamma explains, "but they will let them go to ashrams. So we have church under the guise of an ashram. We can be ourselves and pray to Christ. We are not joining anything or becoming Christian in the sense of church membership.

A second occurence which helped convince Subbamma that she was destined to carry on an evangelistic ministry to caste people was a report by Lutheran church president Samuel Schmitthenner. "If the church is to make an impact upon society in Andhra Pradesh," he wrote, "the gospel must be brought to the Sudhras and higher caste Hindus who make up more than 75 percent of the population." Schmitthenner also noted that because of the patterns of Hindu society, "Religious change can best be brought about

Layman Joseph Allison teaches Bible study in Liberia

through women. The influence of the mother over her sons, daughters-in-law, and grandchildren is very great." Subbamma acknowledges that it is difficult for men to evangelize women in the Hindu culture.

In Liberia, lay ministry takes a different turn. Joseph Allison, a second grade teacher, and James Wolobah, a surgical nurse, have become ordained deacons of the church. They have pastoral authority to baptize and give the sacraments—but only at St. Peter's Church, and not in the whole Lutheran Church in Liberia. The pastor of St. Peter's taught Allison and Wolobah a course in basic Christian doctrine.

Both men are in charge of neighborhood centers in various parts of Monrovia. Their ministry involves visiting and teaching in the centers, as well assisting at St. Peter's Sunday services. On a Tuesday night shortly after 7 P.M., I dropped by the neighborhood center in a section of Monrovia called Sayetown. The community borders on a paved road that leads past the magnificent Executive Mansion and government buildings. But Sayetown has only sandy paths more suited for walking than for cars. Homes and stores are arranged haphazardly, a mixture of shacks and cement walls.

In a tin-roofed, open-air building, I spotted Allison, who had gathered seventeen adults and a host of children around him. He had placed several pictures on a chair and was telling the story of the Ascension. His words flowed as smooth, easy Kpelle, and people listened closely. A single light bulb, suspended on a cord from the rafters, swung gently behind Allison.

Elsewhere in Africa, "people movements" have been the key to lay evangelism. By recognizing that church growth often comes in group fashion, whole communities are received into the fellowship of Christ with minimal disturbance to their culture. Such a group lives in close geographic proximity. They probably speak one language. They may be descended from a common ancestor or group of ancestors. They may have been worshiping one basic superstition.

They may suffer from the same problems—poverty, lack of water, or minimal education. They may earn their living in similar ways and have similar ethical codes. Often the key to a people movement is the conversion of the village chief, or a "medicine man," who is held in high esteem.

In a Barabaig tribe near Lake Balangida in central Tanzania, the medicine man, Langai Shingadeda, finally accepted baptism after fifteen years of arguing with missionaries. When Langai became Christian, he took the name Musa (Moses) which in Swahili means "a leader who takes his people out of darkness." More than that, he agreed to meet with his brother, Paulo, whom he had not spoken to in eight years because of a long-held grudge. Many members of the Barabaig tribe became Christian.

In Japan, gas station attendant Tomezo Ohashi attended a film evangelism meeting in a Baptist church. He had learned about the meeting through the Hokkaido Radio Evangelism and Mass Communication program of the Christian Church. Ohashi's family became aware that his life was changing, and at the gas station Ohashi was given the name of "Smiley." He felt that the gas station was a good place for him to make his witness for Christ. Later he found himself in Tokyo, working with Worldwide Pictures, a film evangelism agency. He now travels widely in Hokkaido and expects to extend his ministry to Okinawa.

On the missionary side, Neil Solvik is a pharmacist who once worked at a corner drugstore in the state of Washington. After a stint at Phebe Hospital in Liberia, he was invited to join the United Mission to Nepal. Solvik accepted the position, realizing that the government of Nepal forbids evangelism. Nepal is a Hindu country, where freedom of religion extends only to Hindus and Buddhists. The government wishes to protect this religious heritage and prohibits outsiders from evangelizing.

Solvik was assigned to Tansen, a one hundred-bed mountain hospital which has only one hour of electricity during the daylight hours each day but which conducts virtually every type of operation, except open-heart surgery or such operations requiring an artificial kidney machine. But Solvik sees himself as an evangelist as well as a pharmacist. "There is no law prohibiting people from talking to each other," he says. "In America, we do most of our evangelizing in groups. One-to-one evangelism has always been the most effective type of witness, and that's the way the church can impact here."

A small Christian church exists in Nepal, and Solvik notes that Tansen had no Christians twenty years ago, but now about sixty Nepalis attend services in Tansen. Most are hospital staff who have heard the gospel from the missionaries/doctors. Those who choose to be Christian in Nepal put their faith and their lives on the line, for some Christians have been imprisoned after being baptized. "Personal evangelism is the door that is open here," Solvik says. "Maybe the restrictions in this country are the Lord's way of forcing us to use the best means of evangelism possible."

Going to Seminary at Home

For lay people overseas who wish to become ordained, "theological education by extension" is an opportunity for them to stay at home and still attend seminary. Appadurai Thangaraj always wanted to be a minister. His father was the pastor of a Congregational church, but when Appadurai graduated from Loyola College in Madras in 1945, family circumstances forced him to get a job. For thirty years he worked at Madras University, moving up through eight promotions to the position of assistant registrar which he held when he retired last year. His son is now a student at the university.

But seven years ago Appadurai began thinking about his upcoming retirement—and his lifelong dream. So he became one of sixty "external B.D. students" at the United Theological College in Bangalore, India who are getting a theological education by extension. TEE, as the program is often called, is an upgraded version of correspondence courses.

To date, Appadurai has completed fifteen courses on subjects such as Introduction to the Old Testament, the Prophets, the Synoptic Gospels, History of the Church of India, Hinduism, and Christian ethics. He has been reading and studying late at night and early in the morning for three to four days a week, and trying to be a father to his three children who still live at home.

Russell Chandran, president of the United Theological College, says, "The more lay people we have in TEE, the more theological renewal we have in the church. Indian lay persons are now in the pietistic, fundamentalistic mold which they receive from the missionaries. Unless the church liberates them, they will not be able to face the changing Indian society."

Despite the popularity of TEE in India, it did not originate there. A Presbyterian seminary in Guatemala started the program about twenty years ago when the church leaders realized that their seminaries had only a few students. It was decided that, since most of the work in the local congregations was being carried out by the older, "natural" leaders of the communities, the professors and even the classes would go to these leaders to instruct them. The program was also designed to avoid the costly and detrimental situation of uprooting the men from their communities. Today, some eighty programs of TEE are educating eleven thousand students in Latin America.

How Many Missionaries?

The extensive ministry by lay people overseas raises the question in North America about the number of missionaries which churches should send abroad. Despite the extensive changes in the world's setting and the nature of the autonomous overseas churches, some North American churches feel that increasing numbers of missionaries must be sent since the world's population continues to increase.

For example, the foreign mission board of the Southern Baptist Convention hopes for 100 percent increase in its missionary force by the year 2000. The church currently has two thousand six hundred missionaries; it wants five thousand by the end of this century. The board is also aiming for a 50 percent rise in the number of countries served by its missionaries, raising the total from the current eighty-one to one hundred and twenty-five. Moreover, the board projects a ten-fold increase in the number of churches in their foreign mission fields—from seven thousand three hundred and thirty-nine in 1975 to seventy-three thousand four hundred by the year 2000.

Projections by most other churches, however, are moving in the opposite direction. A report from the Division of Overseas Ministries of the Christian Church (Disciples of Christ) indicates that they will be using fewer career-type missionaries. "It is not because people who want to serve overseas have less commitment. It is simply that radical changes everywhere, with more and more well-trained leaders developing in all the churches overseas, mean that we cannot promise anybody a life-time career overseas. Our policy now is to appoint persons to specific terms of service (varying from six months to four years) in a particular place to do a particular job on the basis of requests from a church or institution there. We are speaking, therefore, for the most part of short-term or single-term, fraternal-type workers— some of them young, some of them middle-aged, some of them at early retirement."

The Division for World Mission and Ecumenism of the Lutheran Church in America has undergone a sharp reduction in the number of missionary personnel serving overseas in recent years. According to the division's executive director, David Vikner, "the most obvious reasons for this reduction are missionaries being replaced by nationals, government restrictions on the presence of missionaries in certain countries, the inadvisability of too many missionaries serving in a given area, financial stringencies, and the church's inability quickly to find both the proper positions overseas and the right persons to fill these positions. Besides career people and persons for specific positions for longer or shorter periods of time, one must recognize, and if possible, foster the Christian witness potential of LCA lay persons working overseas in a variety of secular occupations."

One noticeable shift in the LCA's overseas personnel is the large number of young people who are serving for short periods of time as teachers, nurses, and working with youth groups. Jeff Littleton of Wisconsin went to Malaysia for three years to teach English in the cities of Grik and Lenggong. "I wanted to get out and do something different," says Jeff. "For the past eight years I worked part time in a clothing store but I had a great desire to be in church work. My generation can have an exciting time working in the church."

Unfortunately, two other factors entered into the decision to send fewer missionaries. One was the revelation in 1975 that the United States' Central Intelligence Agency had been using missionaries as informers. Almost immediately, the credibility of U.S. missionaries was suspect by the very people overseas they had been sent to assist. The CIA's engagement in activities that are prohibited by international law and by Article 6 of the U.S. Constitution—and approved by at least two U.S. Presidents—caused a sharp loss in the moral standing of overseas personnel. The CIA has changed its policy and now prohibits initiation of contact with American clergy and missionaries abroad. The CIA is not prohibited, however, from contacting foreign nationals, nor does it preclude missionaries from volunteering information at home or abroad.

The larger concern over the number of missionaries is financial. A "money revolution" has struck the mission enterprise. For years, it was believed that missionaries sent to "underdeveloped nations" could be supported cheaply because the powerful American dollar worked wonders. For many years, the missionary could live abroad for almost a pittance. By western standards he would be living sacrificially, but in the eyes of the overseas people he was serving, he was living well. This was also the era when a $10 gift might support an orphan for a month and $1,000 would build a church.

Now it has become clear that it costs as much to operate a mission in Taipei, Tokyo, or Hong Kong as it does to begin a congregation in Cleveland or Boston or St. Louis. The cost of living index in Tokyo is 17 percent higher than in New York.

The money crunch becomes apparent when one realizes that the United Church of Christ had three hundred and forty-three missionaries in 1970 and one hundred and eighty-seven in 1975. During those five years, the United Church's Board of World Ministries lost approximately 7 percent of its share of the "national basic support" for the denomination. This meant an average loss of about $125,000 per year over the period, a total loss of nearly $750,000. The United Church's Board of World Ministries receipts in 1975 would have had to more than double the amount received in order to have equalled the purchasing power in 1970, and substantially greater than that to offset overseas inflation. Even so, total receipts for the board in 1975 topped $6,000,000.

In other churches, the Division of Overseas Ministries of the Christian Church (Disciples of Christ) in 1976 had one hundred and fourteen overseas staff and their families serving in twenty-seven countries, with the division budget exceeding $2.4 million. The Presbyterian Church in the U.S. had three hundred and fifty-two missionaries at the end of 1975, with a budget of $5.1 million. The Division of World Outreach of the United Church of Canada in 1965 supported one hundred and thirty mission personnel in nineteen countries, with the division having a budget of $2.1 million. A 10 percent budget cut in 1977 by the General Assembly Mission Council of the United Presbyterian Church will reduce their missionaries from four hundred and three to three hundred and sixty. The number of missionaries being sent out by some eighty mission societies in Britain has dropped by 25 percent during the last four years.

In the Lutheran Church in America, the cost of sustaining missionaries overseas has risen 48 percent in the last five years. In 1969, a missionary unit cost $11,824. By 1977, the cost was $20,490. These figures include salary, children's educational costs, housing, and travel to and from overseas. The reasons for the increased cost are several. The dollar was devalued in some overseas countries; the cost of living increased substantially in many of these countries; the cost of travel rose dramatically. In addition, the percentage of the LCA budget devoted to world mission declined from 25 percent in 1966 to 19 percent in 1976, for a reduction of $5.4 million to $4.4 million. In 1967, it cost $2.5 million to maintain two hundred and eighty-eight missionary units, and in 1975 $3 million for one hundred fifty-eight units. Officials of the LCA's Division for World Mission and Ecumenism have concluded that they cannot financially afford to "be all things to all peoples." Surprisingly, however, the reduction in missionary personnel, coupled with the lessened need for leadership overseas, has meant that those persons deployed by the Lutheran Church in America now serve in more countries than at any time in the church's history. The LCA is now involved in thirty-six countries; in 1963, the figure was sixteen.

The question of "how many missionaries" is still largely dependent upon the situation in overseas churches. But, without question, the talents of lay people are the key to much of the vitality and growth of the church overseas.

5 New Shapes of Mission

Methodist minister Joe Bannerman is well known in the teeming city of Tema, Ghana. Tema was a fishing village of one hundred and fifty mud houses in the early 1950's but today one hundred and two thousand people call it home. As the city's first urban industrial missioner, Bannerman walks the streets and visits factories from 6 A.M. to 10 P.M. There are two hundred and two major business establishments in the city such as Volta Aluminum Company, Ghana Italian Oil Refinery, Tema Steel Works, the Ghana Publishing Company, the Tema Textile Company, and the Cement Works Ghana Limited. The estimated labor force is twenty-seven thousand.

Bannerman has helped the church respond to this new setting for missions. Through workers' fellowships in twelve of the industrial establishments, credit unions have been formed. Budgeting, family planning, and the right use of leisure have been encouraged, and leaders have been trained. A Tema Welfare Association was formed which promoted a cultural festival and fought for lower water rates and better housing for workers.

Nearly halfway around the world from Tema, Queenstown Lutheran Church in Singapore is situated so that thirty-five thousand people can view the steeple from the balconies of their apartments. The brick church building with its sharply sloping roof is encircled by ten-story high-rise apartments that house a hundred families each. Along with a shopping center and a market, the church forms the physical core of the Queenstown community.

"Sunday is actually our slack day," says the pastor. On Sunday the church has English and Chinese Sunday School and church, a coffee hour, pastor's class and evening worship. The street noise that disturbs the worshiper is a constant reminder of the church's location.

But then, on Monday through Friday, a play center for one hundred and seventy neighborhood pre-schoolers is operated in the morning and the afternoon. At other times, Bible study, youth fellowship, classes in sewing, cooking, art, harmonica, adult education, a chess club, Boys Brigade (similar to Boy Scouts), a church softball team, little league basketball and softball, and choir practice occupy the church's facilities.

"See the balcony on that apartment house?" asked Bill Bolm, an American who formerly directed the play center. "Look how narrow it is. Now you see why the church has to provide something for these kids to do." A former football quarterback and coach, Bolm said that "these kids can still play ball when I leave. But if they 'have the word' then I'm thrilled. I look to see who comes to play *and* who comes to Sunday School and church."

These ministries reflect some new shapes of the church in today's increasingly urbanized, industrialized, and westernized world. Urban ministry, for example, was hardly given serious thought two decades ago. But recently, a chart in the office of a missionary in Dar es Salaam, the capital of Tanzania, asked, "Has your church an urban ministry plan?" Then the chart listed these statistics for the city:

1891—14,000 population—2 churches;
1945—39,000 population—10 churches;
1969—300,000 population—60 churches;
1989—1,000,000 population—? churches.

Lloyd Swantz prepared the chart when he was director of the Urban/Industrial Mission of the Christian Council of Tanzania. "We have seventy places of worship to serve approximately one hundred thousand Christians," he said. "If we are to serve four hundred thousand additional

Christians in the next twenty years, we need to build fourteen new churches every year for the next twenty years. Currently we're only building two or three new churches a year."

As a sociologist, as well as urban planner and missionary, Swantz (now in Finland) feels that if the churches in the cities cannot handle the number of Christians who are migrating into urban areas in search of work, "then we must stop baptizing them up-country in their villages. In twenty-five years, there will be more Christians in African cities than in the rural areas."

Furthermore, Swantz estimates that only about one-half of the Christians presently in Dar es Salaam are registered with any church. On an average Sunday, he continues, only about one-fourth of the registered Christians attend services. This means that for every Christian inside the church, three are outside.

To overcome the shortage in the number of churches in Dar es Salaam, Swantz has proposed the "house church." He recognizes that congregations like to have their own building, but realizes that meeting under a tree or on a front porch is an ideal spot for a congregation to begin. When churches begin thinking about building, he suggests that they secure at least two acres of land and that they should consider their future parking needs.

At Saint Peter's Lutheran Church in Monrovia, the capital of Liberia, mushrooming population is also the problem. Even without a special evangelism program, more than one hundred persons are baptized into the church every few months. To serve the rapidly growing population, Saint Peter's has set up neighborhood ministries among concentrations of potential members. Religious instruction is given at these centers, along with literacy training, music education, and worship. Basically the groups are satellites of Saint Peter's congregation, feeding the growth and worship of the main church. When they grow strong enough, they may become separate congregations.

When Lutheran missionaries went to Liberia in 1860, they went through the port city of Monrovia, but did not stop. They went up the Saint Paul River and established churches and schools at twenty-five mile intervals, eventually reaching about 200 miles inland. As a result, nearly ninety years passed before the first Lutheran congregation—Saint Peter's—was established in Monrovia.

The urban setting caused a different situation at the Christian Medical College and Hospital at Vellore, India, when it took a strong stand against an employees' strike in 1975. The hospital, which is supported in part by the United Church of Christ, found that when it fired employees who were involved in corruption at the institution, the state government sided with the strikers. The seventy-day work stoppage cost the hospital $300,000, but the doors remained open, management was ultimately vindicated, and a strong Christian witness against corruption was made.

In Guntur, India, Lutherans own nearly one-half mile along the city's main road. There's the Lutheran Publication House, the office of the president of the Central Guntur Synod, a book store, a library, and a vocational training school. Next is Saint Matthew's Church, a modern structure with a neon-lit cross at night. Beside the church are a number of stores owned by the Andhra Evangelical Lutheran Church. There's a bakery, a milk bar, an underwear shop advertising "new look brassieres" and "tantex" hose, a stationery shop, a novelty corner, a general store, a bank, and a newsstand. These stores pay rent to the church for the occupancy of the property.

Going into Industry

Issei Ogata was a young Japanese soldier during World War II who was assigned to defuse U.S. bombs that failed to explode. When a "dud" suddenly went off in his hands, he was knocked unconscious, blinded, and had his left arm blown off. Ogata was a Buddhist, and was considering suicide when a friend introduced him to a blind

Lutheran pastor. The visit turned around Ogata's life. No one would have predicted that twenty-five years later he would be the pastor of the largest church in Toyota, Japan, and be recognized all over the country as an authority in industrial evangelism because of his contacts in the city of car-making fame.

When the Toyota Motor Company made the jump to assembly line production in 1962, workers came to the plant from all parts of Japan. The city's population jumped from thirty-five thousand to two hundred and thirty thousand and the motor company employed forty-one thousand workers. But production work was new to Japan. Craftsmen who were accustomed to "beginning and finishing" a job were unhappy at turning certain bolts on the metal frames that passed endlessly before them. They became restless and questioned the meaning of life.

Ogata sensed the problems, arranged meetings in homes of Christians so that workers could be invited to them. Ultimately he became a friend of Eiji Toyota, president of the company, and was invited into the factories to speak with the workers. By the time a new church was completed in 1970, Ogata had built such rapport that workers began coming to the church every night. On Mondays, the "seekers" meet to discuss everyday problems such as boy/girl relationships, the meaning of work, and the problems of leisure. On Tuesdays, there are prayer meetings. On Wednesdays, twelve to fifteen workers meet for Bible study. On Thursdays there are crafts. Fridays, the workers bring in speakers on business and politics. On Saturdays there are English classes (Mrs. Toyota attended for a time). Sunday mornings and evenings are devoted to worship, where some of the workers serve as ushers.

South of Toyota, Ryuzo Kamino can see—but he is very sick. He suffers from rice oil poisoning, which means that he is often nauseated, too weak to hold a job, afflicted with diarrhea, swollen joints, discolored nails, numbness of the limbs, and skin eruptions that look like acne.

Kamino charges that he was poisoned by contaminated rice oil produced by the Kanemi Soko Company.

On a bright October day, Kamino went to the main gate of the plant and threw himself onto the concrete pavement, forcing the supply trucks to screech to a halt. Drivers soon milled about, wondering how to remove Kamino. Some of them noticed that he was using a Bible for his pillow on the hard surface. A few weeks before his lie-in, Kamino had been joined in a twenty-four-hour sit-in at the gate by six Lutheran pastors.

Even so, Kamino has had little effect upon the burgeoning water, air, and food pollution that afflicts Japan. Hundreds have been deformed through mercury poisoning. Thousands have asthma from tons of sulphuric acid gas discharged into the air. Milk from one company was found to contain arsenic. Americans visiting Japan are astounded that such pollution and damage to human life are allowed to continue virtually uncurbed. But Japanese industries are geared to turning a profit rather than toward conservation. Legislation protects industry with tariffs, and gives incentives for the enlargement of business. A worker's job, housing, grocery store credit, and even his recreation are often provided by the company, so a worker is hesitant to complain when it might mean the loss of his job.

For these reasons, the Lutheran church in Kurosaki in southern Japan has participated in protests, with members carrying signs and collecting funds for the victims. The pastors—both American and Japanese—speak out against the problem. As for Kamino, he says, "God is still creative in society. Only now, he has a new role for me to play—alerting people to the dangers of pollution."

In Bangkok, Thailand, urban industrial missioner David Eichner finds that his major challenge is not pollution, but rather methods for making life more meaningful for laborers in the sprawling, noisy and hot industrial area of Prapradaeng, south of the city. His "parish" has more than two hundred thousand workers in seven hundred factories. Eichner assists Pastor Samrit Wongsang, a thirty-five-year-old convert from Buddhism, who is a pastor of the Church of Christ in Thailand. During his seminary training, Samrit worked eight hours a day for a producer of laminated flooring. "The president is a Christian," says Samrit, "so he lets me come and talk with the workers now."

Samrit speaks with individual workers, dealing with such problems as low wages, dissatisfaction with labor laws, poor sanitation in company dormitories, and loneliness. Many factory owners will not open their gates to him. They fear that Samrit may organize workers into pressure groups, since Thailand does not currently have trade unions. They don't even like their workers to go to the Bible classes or recreation centers which Samrit operates.

Far away in Sao Paulo, Brazil, Pastors Karl Busch and Ulrich Fischer of the Church of the Lutheran Confession, have set up a "center for the orientation and education of the family." The center is open three days a week and serves one hundred and twenty persons a month.

"We're serving the factory worker and his family," says Fischer. "Most of the counseling is in the area of family problems—child rearing, planned parenthood, divorce." "Industry didn't invite us in," said Busch, a tall blond Brazilian of German background. "They didn't care about their employees' religion. We put up a notice in the town hall and other public places and people began to come."

Of Radios, Schools, and Hospitals

The rhythm of the music is lively, and the words are lyrical in Telugu, one of the languages of southern India.

"Lord Jesus, we join hands and walk with you . . . you have come like a baby, we join hands and play with you . . . we take our writing slates and go to school and you go with us . . . we join hands and walk with you . . . if we walk with you, at the end we will always be with you . . ."

The strains of this children's song are being broadcast

over Suvartha Vani, a studio of the Radio Voice of the Gospel. An Indian pastor, Solomon Raj is in charge of this evangelistic thrust which produces forty-five-minute programs daily for broadcast in India, and similar programs for broadcast four days a week in Sri Lanka (Ceylon). About 30 percent of the programming is religious, Solomon Raj says. "This balance works well because most listeners are non-Christian and would not understand if we broadcast straight Scripture. We want to assist in the total development of people so we have music, devotions, and dramas which deal with the problems of society—marriage, literacy, caste. In this way, we are able to give a Christian perspective to life without quoting 'chapter and verse.'"

A continent away, a sign reading "Lutheran Radio Center" stands straight and tall against the blue African sky. Jamaica-born Bert Mensah who once served there said that he was "just a technician" at the center, but he understated the case. Mensah made the church's word heard in Swahili every day for an hour and a half from the Congo to the Indian Ocean, and from Ethiopia to South Africa.

Along with a Tanzanian program director, Mensah and the center's twelve staff members produced tapes of music, drama, devotions, and religious instruction which are beamed over the Radio Voice of the Gospel. The radio center in Moshi is one of fourteen in Africa, Asia, and the Middle East which prepares tapes for transmission over the radio facility.

The power of radio evangelism is evident when you see Tanzanians walking down the street holding transistor radios to their ears. That's why Mensah spent so much time on safari, recording church choirs in Tanzania, Kenya, and Uganda. "Sometimes we recorded at three places on one day," he says. "And sometimes it took us three days to drive to one place to record." Every Friday, the program includes a Bible study that invites listeners to write for a correspondence course. Over the years, nearly ten thousand people have requested the course.

In Japan, radio evangelism has given way to television evangelism. Each district of the Japan Evangelical Lutheran Church owns television cameras, video cassette recorders and playback units. Congregations videotape special events and share them with other congregations. The tapes are used for information, education, and outreach, often being shown in family groups as well as in churches.

Education has always been a major shape of church mission outreach. Elementary schools have been turned over to the government in some parts of the world as in India, where eight hundred Lutheran schools were given to the government in 1959. By contrast, the boys' and girls' high schools in Kumamoto, Japan, are thriving under the auspices of the church. Interestingly enough, the students not only study, but also provide janitorial services. In Tanzania, where the Lutheran church established schools, 95 percent of the youngsters from Lutheran homes attend, whereas the national average is about 50 percent. Church schools have unknowingly educated Tanzania's leaders.

Many schools, though, could learn from the philosophy of Hansruedi Peplinski, a Swiss-born pastor and educator who is principal of the "Movimiento de Educacion Popular" in Caracas, Venezuela. The 1.5 million dollar layout teaches two hundred and fifty youngsters from age seven through their mid-teens to read, write, and trades such as carpentry, metalwork, mechanical drawing, sewing, and nutrition. The basic intention is to teach youngsters a trade so they can boost themselves our of the slum homes in which they live.

The school's modern red brick buildings stand in sharp contrast to the ramshackle houses nearby. "Some people call me a dreamer," says Peplinski, "but I'm not. I'm very practical. Other agencies are not involved in community work here so the church must be. You can look at the rural people who move into these barrios and get the wrong idea. A slum in the United States is something on the way down. In Caracas it's an area on the way up. This school is important because we try to change the kids from a rural to an urban mentality."

Although medical missions have always been a major part of the church's efforts, two dimensions of that work are especially striking today. One is mental health. The other is leprosy rehabilitation.

It was about noon at Irente Hospital in the Usumbara Mountains of northern Tanzania when the sound of a large bell rang through the mountains. In a few minutes, young men began appearing from all directions. Nearly thirty came in from working in the coffee plantation. Others stopped shelling corn, splitting wood, cracking rocks into gravel, and helping in the carpentry shop to gather around a spigot and wash up for lunch.

"Our aim is for all patients to do some useful work," explained Helmut Scholten, superintendent of the mental hospital. "That's our major form of therapy."

By now, eighty patients had gathered in the small courtyard. On either side were white cement buildings which served as sleeping, eating, and office quarters. I had come to this quietly efficient, but largely unknown Lutheran hospital in Tanzania because it is one of only three or four mental institutions serving this country of twelve and one-half million. Until several years ago, emotionally disturbed patients in Tanzania were usually kept in prison. Now Irente may become part of the nation's plan to establish seventeen psychiatric wards around the country for short-term treatment of mental illness.

With me was the only American at Irente, a Lutheran agriculturist who manages the Irente Farm, 380 acres of rolling countryside which provides therapy for the patients and part of the food and financial support for the hospital.

In many ways, Irente is more of a "home" than a hospital. It does not have extensive medical facilities, and nearly all of the patients are able to care for themselves. "They're schizophrenics, manic-depressives, epileptics, and basically non-violent," says superintendent Scholten. "All of them are referred to us after having been in a government hospital."

Malnutrition is one cause of nervous disorders. Villages are not as tension-free as might be expected. The pace of life is not so much a factor as intrigue from witchcraft and hexes. A man plagued by a mental disorder is likely to think, "who did this to me" rather than "what sickness do I have."

In southern India, I met a leper named Samundi in the village of Nalanganelle. You would never know, however, that he has leprosy. Samundi doesn't have stubs for fingers or stumps for feet. His case was diagnosed ten years ago and a drug named Dapsone has kept it under control.

Samundi is thirty-seven, a Hindu farmer, and has never been to a hospital for his leprosy. But on this day, he was being examined at a clinic from the Schieffelin Leprosy Research Sanitorium. He received a routine checkup—blood smears were taken from his ear lobes and face—and he was given a protective glove for his leprous hand which had developed an open sore from winnowing grain.

Along with fifty others who came to the two-hour clinic, Samundi heard a word of prayer, a brief program on early signs of leprosy, was taught some elementary physical-therapy exercises for maintaining movement in affected limbs, and was examined by a doctor.

Mobile health clinics and village education programs are two of the major medical developments in southern India that makes today's leprosy very different from the biblical images we might have. Early detection, reconstructive surgery, artificial limbs, and occupational therapy are some of the leprosy-fighting efforts at the sanatorium which is, in part, sponsored by the Lutheran Church in America.

"Leprosy work is considerably different than it was twenty years ago," says Ernest Fritschi, surgeon and superintendent at the sanatorium. "We have as many new cases of leprosy each year as we used to, but we catch it earlier. Leprosy as a disease is not the problem; the problem is the neglected case which causes deformity. The deformity then causes the patient to be ostracized from the rest of his community. If he is not deformed, he is still accepted." Fritschi operates on leprosy-deformed hands and feet. Missionary physiotherapist Steve Kolumban helps straighten a patient's "claw" hand through finger exercises and wax baths. Since leprosy attacks the nerves in the arms and legs which control muscle movements and feelings, Fritschi corrects a deformed hand by transplanting a tendon from the patient's leg to his wrist. The ends of the tendons are attached to the affected fingers, a procedure which restores motion to the hand and fingers, but does not correct the loss of feeling.

Into the Bush

Ministry in the Tanzanian bush is unlike ministry anywhere else. First you must ride a big yellow bus south of Arusha for about two hundred miles. The ride takes eight-and-one-half hours. Your knees cramp because African buses have less room between the seats than American buses. At the start, there are seventeen of us on the bus as it leaves Arusha. But by midday there are sixty passengers and 50 seats. And, in the aisle, pumpkin-size fruit, bundles of wood, big cans of water, and tied-up bundles of corn.

The tar road becomes gravel, then sand, mud, and then back to gravel again. In the open field I see several zebras and four ostriches. At one stop a young warrior tries to get on the bus with his spear. The attendant takes it away and throws it on top of the bus.

After the bus ride, a veteran missionary picks me up

NEW SHAPES OF MISSION

in his Toyota land cruiser and we ride seventy-five miles over narrow roads (tracks, they call them, because you follow two beaten-down tire tracks through the grass). We go down rocky slopes and across streams. At one point we stop and I take some pictures. The elephant grass on either side is as tall as the land cruiser.

After several hours, we reach Munguli. In the midst of fields of corn are grass huts so low that you have to stoop to enter. Sticks have been jammed in the ground, intertwined, and elephant grass placed on top. It's cozy inside, and smoky because a fire is always burning, partly for cooking and partly to cure the meat that hangs over it.

Outside the hut, a woman leans over a rocky slab, pours out some corn and grinds it with another stone. In less than thirty seconds, it is cornmeal. The missionary is talking to everyone in sight, and soon introduces me to Daniel, the leader of one segment of the Kindiga tribe. He has leathery feet and sandals with soles made from a discarded rubber tire. A knife sticks out of the back of his belt and he has beads around his head. Daniel tells me that about two hundred adults and one hundred children in the tribe are Christian.

As darkness approaches, Daniel and others in the tribe walk toward the combination school and church which the Central Synod of the Evangelical Lutheran Church in Tanzania helped build. The missionary plans to show a filmstrip of "Daniel and the Lions' Den," projecting the film on the outside wall of the school. I look around wondering where he will plug in the projector, when I see a cord snaking from the projector to the battery of the Toyota. He also shows slides of wild animals and pictures from a previous visit to the Kindigas. They are thrilled to see themselves.

Daniel tells me more about the church. "Our whole way of life has changed," he says. "It used to be a life of hardship. Now we receive clothes from the Central Synod and from overseas (one man was wearing a boy scout shirt from Michigan). When I pray to God, I know God and his angels hear me. We have new hope because we now consider ourselves human beings and the people of God."

The Word Is Holistic

The myriad shapes of church missions are almost too vast to describe—from urban industrial efforts to radio evangelism, to leprosy hospitals to the bush. In these settings, churches are recognizing that each individual must be approached as a whole human being with various needs. A person is a spiritual being who needs to worship; he is an economic being who needs to eat and have a place to live; he is s social being who needs to have the respect of others. If a mission project deals only with the spiritual side of the person, or the economic side, or the social side, without regard for the other sides, the project is inadequate.

These individuals also live in communities with cultures which must be respected. If a mission project changes one aspect of the community, care must be taken not to upset the balance in other parts of the culture. If a community immunizes all of its members, for instance, but does nothing about enlarging the food supply for the increased population that will result from fewer deaths from an illness, the mission project will be in trouble because it did not recognize the interdependence (there's that word again!) of the person and his community.

Mission strategists call such ministry to the total person and the total community "holistic." It is a major reason why the shape of overseas missions is more varied than ever before. No situation is beyond the church's scope. This is in keeping with the example of Jesus who looked upon men and women as persons in need of many things —his forgiving love, food, clothing, medical care, and alterations in the oppressive structures of society. Missions are attempting to follow his pattern.

6 Look at the Church Grow!

Manoel de Mello was born thirty-six years ago in the northeastern Brazilian state of Pernambuco as the twenty-fourth of twenty-five children. During his early adulthood, he was a house painter. But then de Mello turned into a fiery evangelist and began to spread the word instead.

Before long, he founded the *Brasil Para Cristo* Evangelical Pentecostal Church. Today, twenty years after the founding, the church claims an adult membership of more than one million. In 1969, it became the first Pentecostal church to join the World Council of Churches.

"My formal education does not go much beyond learning the ABC's," de Mello admits. "I sat on an empty kerosene box in a one-room elementary school for only a few months." But when he stands on a platform today with his wavy hair and deep-set eyes, he holds his Bible open, jabs the air with his finger and thousands listen. "Our services are more vivid than those of Billy Graham," he says, "more like Oral Roberts. We heal, we get excited. When I preach, I wander around the aisles. The service may last two hours."

Manoel de Mello's "great temple" in Sao Paulo, Brazil, seats twenty-five thousand. In addition, radio programs carry his voice across the country. Sao Paulistas hear him on the air three times daily. At the same time, de Mello points out that he is departing somewhat from the traditional Pentecostal pattern. "We emphaize not only the spiritual but the social as well," he says, mentioning his Brazilian educational center as an example. The center is applying for authorization to begin college-level courses in law, philosophy, and business administration.

Although South America is considered a nominally Roman Catholic continent, Protestants in Brazil grew from about two million in 1945 to nearly twenty million in 1970. Most of the growth came through the Pentecostal movement which de Mello represents. At one time, three thousand new Pentecostal congregations were being founded each year in Brazil.

The Pentecostal surge in South America is only one result of the new shape of missions in a new world marked by urbanization, industrialization, and Westernization. Contrary to current experiences in the United States, Christianity as a world movement has rarely been in better shape. The thirty years since the end of World War II are some of the most remarkable in all of Christian history. The church is actually growing dramatically everywhere in the world except in western Europe, Scandinavia, and the United States. The Third World is not likely to remain third in the number of Christians.

Christians tend to think of the continent of Asia as impenetrable, mostly because of the governments there. But the city of Seoul, Korea, has six hundred Christian churches today. The church in Korea grew more from 1953 to 1960 than it had in the previous sixty years. Medical missionaries in Korea have produced three thousand highly trained medical doctors. In North Korea, communists have wiped out the organized church. But in South Korea there is freedom of worship and some 10 to 13 percent of the population is Christian. According to some observers, Bible training, the cleansing exhilaration of the Spirit, and an emphasis on personal sharing of the faith have set off the spiritual chain reaction. In some areas, personal evangelistic witness is almost as much a requirement of church membership as public confession of faith.

In Malaysia, the Lutheran Church reports a 10 percent growth in 1975, bringing the church's membership to nearly four thousand. In Taiwan, the message is similar. The Presbyterian Church in Taiwan between 1955 and 1965 had a "double the church campaign" and succeeded in its goal.

Indonesia has been the location of one of the most phenomenal mass movements in modern Christian history. All-day services of music, preaching, and one thousand baptisms have often been reported. In one Sumatran village, a service was held at a marketplace with pastors standing in front of the four columns that held up the roof. People who had been instructed lined up in front of the pastors and were baptized. Some five hundred thousand Indonesians have been baptized in recent years, and there are more Presbyterian and Reformed church members in Indonesia than in the United States.

The most rapid growth of Christianity today is in Africa. Some eleven hundred people are converted daily in Kenya, and the church membership growth doubles that of the birth rate in the country which is already more than 50 percent Christian. The Christian Church (Disciples of Christ) reports that in Zaire (Congo) evangelism has caused the church to double its membership in less than ten years, with more than two hundred and fifty thousand members at present. The Mekane Yesus Church in Ethiopia is growing more than 10 percent a year. During a fifteen-day period in 1976, seven thousand seven hundred and seven men, women, and children were baptized in the first mass baptism in the history of the Kembatta synod. Of these, five thousand three hundred and fifteen came from the same parish.

In 1900, 3 percent of the African population was Christian. Today, the figure is 30 percent. Projections indicate that 46 percent of the population will be Christian by the end of the century. Furthermore, Christianity is projected as the major religion of Africa by the year 2000. The center of Christian growth and influence which has shifted from Palestine to Rome to the United States may, by the end of the century, be located in Africa.

Why the Growth?

The church of Jesus Christ always grows because of the impetus of the Holy Spirit. In the past, the Spirit has often been manifested through dedicated missionaries and financial support from church-goers. But the Spirit works in other ways too. Self-reliance and emerging nationalism have been a boon to church growth. When countries become independent and self-reliant, churches want to follow suit. In Kuala Lumpur, Malaysia, a young Christian put it well: "People like to see Christians who are Orientals like themselves, not just Western white Christians."

Politics played an important role in church growth in Indonesia. Many conversions are the result of political expediency. When President Sukarno took over leadership of Indonesia and denounced Westerners, the government turned "pink." The Indonesian communist party infiltrated nearly every village. But after a revolt in 1965, more than two hundred and fifty thousand suspected communists were slaughtered in a political blood bath. The new government interpreted the *Five Principles* of the Indonesian Constitution to include only Christians, Muslims, and Hindus. Tribal customs and animism were not recognized as official.

Many people became Christian as a show of faith in the new government. They knew that "if you're Christian, you're not communist." Sometimes entire villages were baptized and a sign was placed at the entrance, "This is a Christian village."

Sociology was also influential in Indonesian church growth. In the mid-1960's, many Indonesians began to migrate from the agricultural hinterlands to the coastal urban areas, leaving behind not only their homeland but their "home" religion. United Methodist missionary Richard E. Brown explains that "tribal worship depends on a closed community. But urbanization opens up a community." As a result, Christianity is identified with progress and modernity and offers the security people have

Day care center spurs church growth in Singapore

to leave behind when they forsake the villages. In order to reestablish their identity and community, people turn to the church in their new urban setting. In one community where residents thought the spirit of their ancestors lived in a banana tree, a festival was arranged as a farewell to the old religion, a kind of saying "excuse us" to the religion of their ancestors. After that, the people of the community were baptized.

Emotion is the key to growth in South America. Manoel de Mello says that "traditional churches cannot attract the South American masses. The Brazilian temperament is different from that of the European. Our people like crowds and noise and emotion."

That is one reason why Brazilians and people in other countries of South America like *Umbanda*, a form of spiritism that is a strange mixture of African and Indian tribal rites, superstition, and the veneration of saints so characteristic of Portuguese Catholicism. Umbanda focuses on "white magic," imploring the good spirits as well as "black magic," placing curses and hexes on those in disfavor. In Rio de Janeiro, there are seven hundred and sixty-four Christian churches but seven thousand and five hundred Umbanda centers.

The transition from Umbanda to a Pentecostal worship is made easily. Both focus on emotion, healing, ecstasy, and participation. Both tend to be favored by the large lower class, many of them undereducated and economically marginal. In addition, the formality of the Roman Catholic Church and the mainline Protestant churches do not appeal to these masses. The Pentecostals seem to have greater affinity with the poor—and there are a great many poor people in South America. The Pentecostal pastor is usually "from the people and among the people" and not highly educated.

Two Unsolved Problems

Although there are virtually no countries in the world where the gospel has not been preached, it is well to remember that certain groups of people within a country often have been more exposed to Christianity than others. A computer-compiled survey prepared by the Missions Advanced Research and Communication Center of Monrovia, California, has identified four hundred and thirteen distinct groups of "unreached peoples." Of these, more than one hundred and twenty groups with a total population of about two hundred and forty-eight million are said to be "open to change" with respect to religious beliefs. Some thirty-five groups with a total population of more than twelve million were reported to have little or no Christian witness available to them. Some groups are very small—such as three hundred and twenty-five members of the Bororo group in Brazil.

The survey takes seriously the ethnic make-up of countries. For example, Indonesia is 7 to 10 percent Christian. However, certain groups of the population have much higher percentages of Christians. The Batak people make up 3 percent of the population, but nearly 80 percent of the Bataks are Christian. By contrast, Javanese make up 50 percent of the population but less than 5 percent of them are Christian. In the same vein, the tribal peoples of South Vietnam make up 10 percent of the population but are 80 percent Christian. The Vietnamese who make up 85 percent of the population are about 12 percent Christian. This seems to suggest that certain areas of the world have not been evangelized as well as others.

A second concern is the remaining Christian witness in mainland China. The dean of the Chinese Graduate School of Theology in Hong Kong said last year that Christians in China remain loyal to Christ despite being "separated from their western roots and loyalties, deprived of full-time pastors, and without national organization or church buildings."

Other reports are not so optimistic. The Vatican newspaper *L'Osservatore Romano* has written that "there is not even a remote possibility" that the five to six hundred

Roman Catholic priests in the People's Republic of China "are able to practice their ministry. Some of the bishops have been in prison since 1958 and nothing has been heard of them for years. Only about ten of the native bishops who were legitimately consecrated before 1957 are still alive."

Although the newspaper said "There are still Catholics who practice their beliefs," they can practice them "only in private." At the time of the revolution in 1949, the Vatican estimates that three and a half million Chinese were Roman Catholics. But five thousand foreign missionaries were expelled, and church members began to be harassed and church-related institutions were shut down.

The Vatican assessment is consistent with reports by Arne Sovik, director of the study of other faiths and ideologies of the Lutheran World Federation. Sovik says there is no firm evidence that any churches in the country are open except for a Catholic cathedral and a Protestant church, both in Peking. Christian worship takes place in private homes. Some pastors make visits, he continues, but much of the Christian tradition is carried on by lay leaders. Some Christian books are reportedly transported into the country and some radio broadcasts get through.

These two problems have an effect on the growth of the overseas churches. But when they are seen against the backdrop of the varied styles of ministry, the peoples in so many different situations being served, and the growth in the number of the world's Christians, there is still good reason for optimism and even unbridled joy at the impact which the church is having through its "mission in a new world." The "missionary-sending" nineteenth century may be considered by historians as the heyday of the mission enterprise, but future historians will have to give the twentieth century high marks for the church growth that developed from those earlier efforts.

7 What Is the Future?

The event at the Berekum Presbyterian Church in Ghana was history-making. Thirty-six-year-old Dora Ofori Owusu was being ordained as the first woman pastor in the Presbyterian Church in Ghana. The church had not officially approved the ordination of women, but Pastor Owusu was given an exception so that she could become a missionary in the United States for two years. Currently, she is an educational missionary in the Atlanta Presbytery of the Presbyterian Church is the U.S., concentrating on broadcasting and teaching African culture at Atlanta University.

Pastor Owusu is one indication that the future of church missions may lie in the increasing interchange of ideas among people and cultures. At first glance, that approach does not seem to break new ground. But closer observation indicates that many overseas churches are feeling their missionary muscles and are beginning to send missionaries to the United States. Furthermore, they are sending missionaries to other countries as well. The Japan Evangelical Lutheran Church, for instance, has supported a Japanese missionary in Sao Paulo, Brazil, for a number of years. Sao Paulo has the largest concentration of overseas Japanese of any country. The Japan overseas mission which was begun by American Lutherans in 1893 has matured to the point where it now sends its own missionaries to other countries.

Beyond the exchange of missionaries, the future of missions shows increasing dialogues between Christians and Buddhists, Muslims and even communists. There are also new directions in the church's involvement in political situations concerning human rights. But this is to get ahead of the story.

When Pastor Jacob Mugo and his wife, Helen, and their two sons, were commissioned as missionaries of the Presbyterian Church in East Africa, the Mugo family immediately left Kenya to spend a year in the Hudson River Presbytery in New York. "I'm going to the United States as an ambassador not only for the Presbyterian church but also for the African church and Kenya in particular," Mugo said. "I expect to meet church leaders and address different groups while carrying on normal pastoral duties in the presbytery. I shall aim at giving these groups a true picture of Christianity in Africa as well as highlighting some of the problems facing churches in Africa."

Elsewhere in Africa, the Mwanza Town Choir, a Christian group from Lake Victoria in Tanzania, made a "preaching tour" in West Germany. When the leader of the choir was asked why his group went to preach in a Christian country like Germany, he replied, "There are many people born in Christian communities who do not have a Christian commitment. I believe many people in Germany were deeply touched after listening to our songs, testimonies, and sermons." Three Lutheran pastors from Tanzania went to another "Christian" country—the United States, serving congregations in Colorado, Indiana, and Virginia.

These efforts provide cultural cross-fertilization and an exchange of views. Americans do not hold all the world's theological secrets, and mission churches are anxious to share their gospel insights with the rest of the world. These visitors have not been timid in sharing their observations either.

One group, which came under the Lutheran World Federation's "Mission to Six Continents" program, said the churches in the United States were "captives of their culture." Annette Nuber of West Germany told Americans

Tanzanian pastor assists in confirmation at Colorado church

that they "are in danger of becoming a real 'state church' in spite of your system of voluntarism. The church has at many points conformed to the government, while a certain distance is necessary to keep the church as church and the government as government."

Lothar Hoch of Brazil agreed that the U.S. church "does not have the necessary distance and objectivity to be prophetic. It's too much a part of the system." Mrs. Renuka Somasekhar, principal of the Women's College in Madras, India, observed that American churches do not question the values of society. She was "overwhelmed" by the material power which she saw, but felt that Americans are judged more often by what they have rather than by what they are.

Other visitors, such as Manas Buthelezi of South Africa, expressed concern because most Americans seemed ignorant of the struggle against apartheid in Southern Africa. Yoshiro Ishida of Japan added that he found a "feeling of isolationism" and indifference to overseas affairs among Americans.

A Methodist from Bolivia told the National Evangelism Symposium of the United Church of Christ that America is a difficult mission field because most people think they have either accepted or rejected the gospel without really understanding it. Mortimer Arias asked, "How can you evangelize millions of Christians who assume that they have received the gospel and that they are bearers of the good news but who are not at all excited about it?" The Bolivian said that certain types of evangelism in the United States were counterproductive, referring especially to the "sometimes unscrupulous manipulation of feelings, the sentimentality, the superstition, the ideological use of religion, the legalistic and scholastic handling of the Bible, and the cheap presentation of the gospel of so many television programs."

Odhiambo Okite of Nairobi, editor of the East African Christian newspapers *Target* and *Lengo*, referred to himself as a missionary to North America during his visit. In talking with a Canadian seminary professor of world missions, the professor said, "You know, I believe you Africans may very well have great success with the American Indians. They hate us, you know, and who can blame them for that? Maybe you can speak to them." Okite later wrote that the frontiers of mission in North America lie in relating effectively to the historic experiences of blacks, Indians, and Hispanics. "What has this Christian continent done to these people, and what can Christianity possibly mean for them after all of that?" he said. "Black and red theologies are helping liberate the American church from its guilt, giving it a new vision for a new future as one people 'under God.'"

Not all the overseas ambassadors were negative. The "Mission to Six Continents" group was impressed by the efficiency and diversity of American churches. "The congregations seem to be alive," said West German Annette Nuber. "Many people attend the services and come to communion—far more than in my country. People are ready to give money, time, and strength to their congregation."

"Your church bureaucracy is excellent," said Waldo Villalpando of Argentina. "We are highly impressed by your use of the mass media and by your willingness to listen to our criticisms." Others noted that American churches seem ready to tackle new problems as they arise. They were enthusiastic about the special ministries they saw on campuses, in nightclubs, and among apartment dwellers.

Such "missionaries in reverse," many of them from the Third World, are now ministering in Australia, Canada, England, France, Greece, Portugal, and the United States. A report in *Christianity Today* indicates that two hundred and nine agencies in the Third World are sending out three thousand four hundred and eleven missionaries. The top three countries, according to the number of missionaries being sent, are Nigeria with eight hundred and twenty, India with five hundred and ninety-eight, and Brazil with five hundred and ninety-five.

The concept of Third World missions has a longer history than might be expected. Few people are aware that the evangelization of West Cameroon in Africa was pioneered by missionaries from Jamaica in the 1830's. Missionaries from Burma went to Thailand in the same period. The Bataks of Indonesia sent missionaries to Malaya in 1930. To complete the circle, it should be noted that the Lutheran Church in America began missionary efforts in Malaya in 1953, organizing the church in 1963. Now, the mission committee of the Lutheran Church in Malaysia and Singapore expects to take up its first world mission work in 1977, sending missionaries to such countries as Taiwan, Indonesia, Sabah, New Guinea, or the Philippines.

Dialoguing with Other Faiths

Two twenty-eight-year-old television producers were talking with a Christian over dinner in Matsuyama, Japan. The trio had agreed that they wouldn't talk religion. "Our fathers are Buddhist," the producers said, "but we have no interest in religion. Temples, shrines, or churches have nothing to say to us. Christ, now, that's different. There's the ideal of true man who lives for others. I can't understand why Americans, who are Christian, are doing such a poor job of being Christians in their own country or in the world. Our ideal is Christ." Suddenly the conversation had taken an unexpected religious turn. The trio all had further engagements for the evening and expected to conclude dinner at 8 P.M. But at 10 P.M., the proprietor of the restaurant came to the table and whispered regretfully that he would like to go home. The two Buddhists and the Christian then went to a cafe and continued to talk until 2 A.M., discussing Bonhoeffer, Tillich, and Bultmann and the difference between humanism and Christianity.

78

Such interfaith dialogues are common these days but they are usually more structured. In Hyderabad, India, fourteen mission groups support the Henry Martyn Institute of Islamic Studies. The institute interprets the gospel to Muslims through literature and Bible correspondence courses, and helps Christians understand Islam through summer schools, lectures, teaching in seminaries, a quarterly bulletin, and residential training. At the heart of the work are the interfaith dialogues which are held each year, with four Muslim and four Christian scholars presenting papers and discussing them.

At a seminar on "faith and works," the two groups affirmed that faith must be followed by works. But the Christians learned that the Muslims had difficulty understanding the Christian viewpoint of atonement *and* good works because the Muslims feel that good works *are* the atonement. "The Muslims agree that Christ died and that the sins of the believers are forgiven," says S.V. Bhajjan, a Methodist who directs the institute. "But they feel that Christians then are free to do whatever they like—and they point to the low moral standards of the West as evidence. The Christians do not want to confront the Muslims with the faults of Islamic society," continues Bhajjan, "so we say that in this age, all religions suffer from the influence of modern ideologies. We emphasize the importance of serving all humanity in spite of the corruption—which is what Jesus did."

At another dialogue, the subject was the nature of man. "The Muslims feel that man was created weak and that something went wrong," Bhajjan said, "but they do not call it 'original sin' as we do. Our response to them indicates that a child is not born a sinner, but that in a world of sin, human beings cannot escape sin. We also say that society is affected by this sin, and the Muslims can understand that."

Bhajjan is emphatic that "dialogue means that I am willing to sit and listen to my Muslim friend. It means that we share religious experiences because we believe in the same God and the experiences we have in understanding him can be shared. We know him in various ways—the Muslims through a book which reveals the will of God (the Koran), and Christians through the person who reveals God's will (Christ). In this way, the dialogues put the claim of Christ before them."

Elsewhere, the dialogues are between Christians and communists. The Evangelical Presbyterian Church of Portugal has sponsored study conferences throughout the country on "Marx and Paul." A few years ago, some three hundred Roman Catholics and Protestants were members of "Christians for Socialism" in Chile. Small groups related to the organization met in various places. In a tiny shack in Valparaiso, Chile, a Roman Catholic priest often held discussions with twenty-five people. The people lived in the surrounding slum neighborhood. Some were active members of the priest's parish. Some were active members of the Communist Party. Some were both. A statement from the organization read, "Socialism offers hope for a more complete man, and at the same time a more Christian man—that is to say, a man more conformed to Jesus Christ, who came to liberate the oppressed."

Often the dialogues were held in unexpected places. Catholic priests sometimes plowed and planted in the fields. They walked the streets of the slums, taught school, and worked in factories. It was there—in the fields and factories—that the Christian-Marxist dialogues took place. They were not dialogues across conference tables, but situations where deeds spoke louder than words. In these dialogues, many communist members were surprised to discover that true religion is not the opiate of the people, as they had been taught. And many Christians were just as surprised to learn that not all communists are tyrants and anti-religious, as they had been taught.

Interfaith dialogues present some risk to the Christian message, since few people like to be rebuffed. But the dialogues are also a challenge. Bishop Lesslie Newbigin of England, who has spent most of his ministry in India, says there are three basic points to remember in inter-faith dialogue:

1. We participate in dialogue with persons of other faiths believing that we and they share a common nature as those who have been created by one God who is the Father of all, that we live by his kindness, that we have a common responsibility to him, and that he proposes the same blessing for us all.

2. We participate in dialogue as members of the body of Christ—that body which is sent into the world by the Father to continue the mission of Jesus.

3. We participate in dialogue believing and expecting that the Holy Spirit can and will use this dialogue to do his own sovereign work, to glorify Jesus by converting to him both the partners in the dialogue.

Liberation Theology

Beyond the dialogues, "new" theologies are springing up which influence world mission. Most notable is "liberation theology," which has received much of its impetus from Father Gustavo Gutierrez of Lima, Peru. He defines liberation theology as "a global and unique process through which persons become free, assume their proper destiny and become sons of God and brothers of men. There are dimensions in this global process, and one of them is the dimension of political liberation and liberattion of all the other dimensions of man. It means liberation from oppressive governments . . . from hunger and poverty . . . and from the exploitation of a social class by other social classes."

"Revelation does not speak to us only of God," Gutierrez continues, "it simultaneously speaks to us of man. It speaks to us of a God who puts his foot in history. When we attempt to make liberation theology, we take into account the indissoluble link between God and man. It tries, like all theology, to illuminate the Old Testament with the New. It seems to me that liberation theology gives preferential attention to the meaning of life, death, and resurrection of Christ."

To many Americans, though, liberation theology seems left-wing. Porfirio Miranda, a professor of political philosophy at Metropolitan University in Mexico City, told a liberation theology conference in Detroit that the Bible had a strong basis for socialism, citing Acts 4:32: "The group of believers was one in mind and heart. No one said that any of his belongings was his own, but they all shared with one another everything they had."

"It was not Marx who invented that," Miranda said. He does not believe socialism is the ultimate political system, but said that under socialism there would be "no starvation, no inequalities, no injustices—at least no clear injustices and inequalities." He continued that the Christian way of life is opposed to the "individualistic traditions" of capitalism. "I cannot understand how the Christian can be individualistic, how he can fail to care for the poor, for the people who suffer. Christ came to change the world in favor of the poor, the orphans, the widows, the oppressed—and any other interpretation of Christianity is false."

In response, Robert McAfee Brown, a United Presbyterian theologian, said he found liberation theology "exciting" in its view of the Bible as a contemporary document. "We should read Exodus and find maybe we're the Pharaohs," he said. "We desperately need the insights of Latin Americans to be aware of how we are destroying our sisters and brothers elsewhere through American foreign policy and our own Christian complicity with it."

"But such theology is not a savior," Brown continued. "Latin American theologians, with all their merits, are still sexist. Black theologians do not take economic analysis seriously enough and feminist theologians have not clearly related the women's struggle to the class struggle."

Black theology has its influence in Christian missions because, in the words of Alphaeus Zulu, Anglican bishop of Zululand, "It represents the black man's effort to understand and describe the significance to, and relevance for, black people of the God 'whose glory shines in the face of Jesus Christ.' The purpose of black theology is to lead black people to see that when white people treat blacks as less than human, they are being unfaithful to the revelation of God in Jesus Christ. Black theology seeks to help black men understand that in proclaiming release for prisoners, recovery of sight for the blind, and the liberation of broken victims, the Christian's God aims in fact to set the black man free of the white man's fetters."

But the bishop warns that proponents of black theology must not give the impression that such theology should be the handmaid of black revolution, and that such revolution should be violent. God must not be seen as being "for blacks and therefore against whites," he continued.

Americans may not be happy about these expressions of theology from the Third World. But mission proponents cannot avoid coping with such expressions. Twenty-two Third World theologians from twenty countries organized last year at the University of Tanzania "to discuss quite frankly the kind of world we live in." C.T. Vivian, a Baptist professor at Shaw University Divinity School in Raleigh, N.C., the only American attending the conference, pointed out that a paper produced at the meeting suggested that a principle cause of underdevelopment in the Third World is the "systematic exploitation of their peoples and countries by the European peoples," and that "the Christian churches were in a large measure an accomplice in this process."

Human Rights and The World Council

During Christmas of 1975 the Korean National Council of Churches began a week's prayer campaign to protest the arrest of more than two hundred Christians, students, journalists, and academicians who were accused of political dissent. A Roman Catholic poet was being tried as a communist infiltrator in the Korean Roman Catholic Church. Similar human rights crusades by church groups in the Philippines and some Latin American countries are bringing clergy and congregations into bitter conflict with the governments of their countries.

But in Africa, Christian churches which were once depicted as paternalistic agents of colonialism are now being applauded by black Africans for their role in challenging white rule and for their efforts in assisting black states. "The churches have spread more revolution on this continent than Che Guevara, Lenin and Mao Tse-tung," a young Zambian politician said. When his assessment was passed on to a Spanish priest in Rwanda, the priest responded, "Why not? We've been in the business much longer."

Two of the four major black nationalist leaders in Rhodesia, Bishop Abel Muzorewa and the Rev. Ndabaningi Sithole, are Methodist ministers. The presidents of Liberia and Malawi are ministers, and Zambian President Kenneth Kuanda is a lay preacher. In Kenya, President Jomo Kenyatta has asked missionaries to return to the schools and hospitals which were formerly nationalized and from which missionaries were ousted.

"You have to understand," said Canon Burgess Carr, the head of the All-Africa Conference of Churches, "that for the generation of men now in power, the churches provided the only opportunities available."

At the same time, dealing with exploitation and racism has probably brought the World Council of Churches more criticism than any of its many activities. Churches differ on what constitutes their witness to Christ as Lord in the area of political action. When the WCC instituted the Program to Combat Racism in 1969, it could hardly have anticipated the headlines that were to come. Even though WCC officials insisted that financial grants from the program were used only for such humanitarian purposes as medicine and education, rumors circulated that the receiving groups—many of them "freedom fighters" in

Mozambique and other African countries — used the church's money to buy arms. By 1974, the program had distributed $1 million, including grants to some groups in the United States, such as $21,000 to the American Indian Movement to pay for legal aid.

In 1976, Cynthia Wedel, an Episcopal lay woman who is one of the WCC's six presidents, accused the government of South Africa of the "misconception" that the WCC allegedly pays for military supplies for revolutionary groups in Africa. "None of our people who have been on the scene has said the money has gone to promote violence," Wedel said. "It has been largely the government of South Africa that has spread stories that the money went for guns and ammunition."

The council has also been accused of harboring communists. Again, Wedel said "so many Americans say the council must be bad because there are people in it from the communist countries. What they don't understand is that there are no communists in the World Council, only Christians who happen to live in communist lands. When people want to join the council, we don't ask what their politics are."

Because the WCC constitutes a considerable force within the structures of the world's churches, its existence cannot be taken lightly. When the first assembly of the WCC was held in 1948, Christians from eight nations and one hundred and forty-seven member churches gathered. At that time, there was considerable feeling that little could be done about "man's disorder" without direct divine intervention. Yet delegates felt that with God's help, some dent might be made in solving the world's thorny problems in the aftermath of World War II. By the time of the second WCC assembly in 1954, the world's churches had increased in mutual confidence and affection.

At the 1961 assembly in New Delhi, the Russian Orthodox Church and some Pentecostal churches participated as members for the first time, emphasizing the council's oneness rather than its fragmentation. This feeling became apparent at the next assembly in 1968 when seven hundred delegates from two hundred and thirty-five member churches (almost one hundred more churches than were represented at the first assembly) debated the Vietnam War, student rebellions, and the assassination of Martin Luther King without seeing the council's camaraderie disintegrate. Then in 1975, the first WCC assembly in Africa brought larger delegations of women and youth than any previous gatherings, and found new strength in raising such questions as the oppression of Christians in the Soviet Union. Any mission strategy, developed in this decade or the next, must take into account the expressions of the world's Christians as they are enunciated at such gatherings. Such sensitivity is part of "interdependence."

Our Response

If interdependence is the basic philosophy of mission and ecumenical efforts, and lay people and dialogues are having great influence in the shaping and growth of missions in the "world that is our home," what then should our response be as American mission-minded Christians?

First, recognize the **changes** that are occurring. Become familiar with terms such as *self-reliance, partnership*, and *interdependence*. Be open to the rampage of urbanization and the changing sociology of the world.

Second, accept the **challenge** of the new mission strategy. Consider what the churches of the world have to teach us in America. Be prepared to "let go" of "our" mission fields and sit down with our fellow Christians and learn from them as equals in Christ. Give an ear to their theologies.

Third, rejoice in this time of **cheer** for the rapid growth of the church throughout the world. God's word is being spread. It is taking root and producing. God receives the glory and men and women come into his saving grace. Thanks be to God!